YOU'RE HISTORY

YOU'RE HISTORY

THE TWELVE STRANGEST WOMEN IN MUSIC

LESLEY CHOW

Published by Repeater Books

An imprint of Watkins Media Ltd

Unit 11 Shepperton House

89-93 Shepperton Road

London

N1 3DF

United Kingdom

www.repeaterbooks.com

A Repeater Books paperback original 2021

1

Distributed in the United States by Random House, Inc., New York.

ISBN: 9781913462314

Ebook ISBN: 9781913462352

Printed and bound in the United Kingdom by TJ Books Limited.

For D3000, the Stupendous One

CONTENTS

WHY ALL WOMEN

The artists I write on at length in this book happen to be women. A few are truly respected; a good deal more are regarded as guilty pleasures, too tuneful for acclaim. Some are considered fashion-plates or pop cultural jokes. Others, such as Chaka Khan, are seen as wonderful forces of nature with little authorial agency.

What these artists have in common is that they are all anomalies: pioneers in the making, whose output has been too strange for the culture to fully digest. While the greatness of Khan, Neneh Cherry, and even TLC has been acknowledged, these women are not influential *enough*. One reason may be that most of them are not primarily word-based: there is verbal innovation, but it is the kind that comes across sung rather than spoken or written. A monologue is easier to dissect than a landscape of shifting voices, which explains why in-depth writing on Cherry is hard to come by.

There is a shortage of serious, long-form writing when it comes to hip-hop, R&B, and pop, particularly female performers. Cherry and TLC's Lisa Lopes mine dissonance and ugliness in the name of pop, rather than an overtly experimental genre — a risky endeavor unlikely to spawn trends. Hundreds of rock bands have appropriated the chord changes and flat affect of Joy Division, but it is harder to channel the spirit of Lopes, whose rapping combines multiple voices of indeterminate gender and source. Lopes and Cherry remain outliers, marking moments where the culture might have swerved to incorporate their influence, but somehow contrived not to.

Even Kate Bush, whose mastery is never questioned, is renowned more for her eloquence and historical narratives than the pop sensibility that makes such a striking match with her "timeless" themes. There is the assumption that musical influences are guided by taste and logic, that one has a say in the genre of one's own genius. However, tracing influence is not just a matter of looking at immediate social background or zeitgeist. Despite the claims of traditional biography, what hooks a singer's ear may be the addictive hard note in a newsreader's voice, rather than the legacy of her Scandinavian or Afro-Caribbean roots. At a time when references tend to be clearly flagged and respectably eclectic, it is vital to acknowledge the imaginative leaps that an artist can make: out of time, out of milieu, out of mind.

Why are there still relatively few books about pop, compared to the canonical body of literature on rock? Do pop fans tend to work out their notions of rhythm on the dancefloor rather than the page? Is instant melodic pleasure regarded as cheap? Or is there the lingering perception that pop caters to the desires of teens, thereby exposing the author to ridicule? The critic Sheila O'Malley has pointed out that, when it comes to adolescent fans of pop, "their screams of ecstasy are ignored or mocked. But teenage fans picked out Elvis Presley, they picked out Sinatra ... Maybe, instead of belittling teenage girls' frenzies, we should follow the sound to see what the fuss is about."

My goal in writing this book was to "follow the sound" with curiosity rather than derision: to track anything that the ear picks out as striking and memorable, regardless of reputation. It can be tricky to decipher emotions that feel private and fugitive, even though they are provoked by objects that are unquestionably commercial. I have explored pop songs that are potent in spite of their seeming lyrical banality. This involves trying to understand the emotive effects of timbre, noticing how the meaning of words changes on contact with the bass and, most importantly, determining where the *heat* of a song is located. As the composer David Schiff has noted, a song can contest its lyrics and reveal itself through the "warmth of the melodic lines, and musical wisdom always trumps verbal wit." Listening closely to pop means marveling at how pitch, rhythm, and intonation come together in a way that is precisely right yet difficult to fathom — all those little miracles that pop does so brilliantly.

In particular, I want to advocate for urgency and pleasure, so my focus is on performers whose effect on the body is hot, explosive, and immediate, rather than those who adhere to typical standards of refinement and class, such as Grimes and Joanna Newsom, and who are more likely to be celebrated as a result. The artists in this book deal in moods that are generally considered undesirable: an insistent fakeness, emotional dishonesty, uncontrolled sexuality, strident superficiality. Their music tends to grate rather than soothe.

Shakespears Sister go beyond quirky and play with images of the grotesque, envisioning love as a form of witchy possession — a theme that has recently been taken up by the most unlikely of artists: Taylor Swift. Rappers Azealia Banks, Lisa Lopes, and Nicki Minaj similarly work with gut levels of repulsion, testing out the power of feminine sleaze. Banks, Lopes, and Minaj incur serious violations of taste, in a way that more consistently acclaimed musicians such as Janelle Monáe rarely do. They are anomalies in that their songs leave an acrid taste in your mouth — they are drawn to working with disgust and abject topics. They risk sounding shrill. All of the artists in this book are unpalatable, in one way or another. Even the loveliest voice among them, Sade, has oddities that discomfit the listener.

You're History deals with English-language artists, most of whom have enjoyed at least a degree of chart success. In part, this is to draw attention to the fact that music can be ubiquitous yet underrated. Pop, by and large, is still seen as foolishly infectious — the cultural equivalent of junk food or fast fashion. The critical focus seems to be on removing the contagion as opposed to explaining *why* it catches on. Therefore, a song as strange as Rihanna's *Umbrella* or Janet Jackson's *Nasty* can attain universal recognition while the secrets of its power remain untapped.

The innovative film critic Judith Williamson always preferred reviewing mass-market movies to little-seen masterpieces: her theory was that she wanted to find out what it took to strike "the right chord" with the public, rather than searching for the marginal or the underground. In a similar way, this book seeks to identify the elements of a song that touch a nerve; I have only included one chapter on a singer whose work is relatively obscure, Michelle Gurevich. I look at several artists – Minaj, Rihanna, Sade – who are fascinating despite reputation. These women may be well-known but they are critically under the radar, their peculiarity masked by popular success. While Jackson and Khan are considered great performers, their songs seldom receive the close analysis they deserve, unlike the work of the introspective, indie songwriter.

A pop smash may be written off as a spark of serendipity or dumb luck, but it is a formula of pleasure that has yet to be perfected. Record companies do not have full control over what hits home and produces love. This is because memorable songs have a necessary component of strangeness that is hard to calculate. What lifts a song into greatness may be a singer's impulse to lengthen, slur or skip over a note, or an incorrect turn of phrase that nonetheless becomes iconic. Effects like these interrupt the concept of the songwriter as a single identity and authority. It is tough, if not impossible, to consciously build such whims into a song's structure: they are more often discovered during rehearsal, the evidence of a quirk not resisted.

I found it particularly challenging to come to terms with the complexity and contrary nature of TLC, Jackson, and Banks. On their debut album, TLC encompass an astonishing range of sounds and attitudes: their songs combine the macho posturing of punk with 1960s girl-group sweetness. Skipping between hip-hop, R&B, pop, and funk without ever settling on a genre, the record is constantly on the move, surprising us with musical twists and sudden mood changes. Bragging lyrics and harsh effects give way to moments of introspection: the women are just as fierce in describing their passions as in attacking their detractors. In contrast to most of their contemporaries, from SWV, Brownstone and Jade to Destiny's Child, who tend to present a rational, unified front, TLC give us multiple, jostling perspectives. The songs come across as mercurial, alarming, and vulnerable: a series of mixed messages designed to unsettle.

What's amazing is that TLC did of all this in plain sight: they are America's best-selling female group. While the band seems as determined to smash boundaries as, say, Nina Hagen, they are not obviously avant-garde: they present us with threatening voices, but do so under the guise of sassy, mainstream pop. This may be the reason why they were able to take so many niche sounds and bring them to the center of 1990s culture.

This book is an argument for the cheap, the shrill, the coarse, the sour, the pungent, the saccharine: for any off-putting effect as long as it is memorable. I looked for songs that have been critically discounted but continue to boggle the mind, for emotional tones that are "nasty" (in the Janet Jackson sense of the word) rather than balanced, and for the one-off hit more than the tempered masterpiece. Above all, I wanted to pay an overdue tribute to the best "oohs" in the business.

DEVIL YOU KNOW:
THE SECRETS OF POP

What do the lyrics of pop songs mean? For instance, if a song insists on delivering the same message over and over again, what does that suggest? Depending on the melody, repetition could mean exhaustion or reinforcement – it could be urging us either to pass over the words or penetrate them. And if, say, the last word of the chorus was underscored by a beat that was slightly mysterious – it kicked up in a way we didn't expect – what would happen then? Would we still take in the verbal message – or would we simply coast over it, arrested by the rhythmic strangeness? In this case, it's really up to the arrangement to decide what a song "intends," rather than the lyrics. Whether it's a guitar that brings black smudges to mind, or a tinny sound that emphasizes its own cheapness, music is full of effects that are hard to explain, but what they have is an emotional clarity that words can't override.

When we infer depth in music – when we sense a song parting to reveal the bassline beneath, like a section of exposed wiring – it's as if we're receiving a code that tells us how to treat the lyrics. Even a fairly cheesy track can be arresting if it implicitly tells you to disregard its "content" by advancing the melody at all costs. In album reviews, it's common to see songwriters dismissed for clichéd wording, without any information about how those words come across rhythmically: how a particular phrase is leaned on, or made strange through a quirk of intonation. This kind of intimate attention is particularly necessary when writing about hip-hop, where words can be fired up or deadened by their inflection, an effect that would be lost on the page. It doesn't make sense to quote lyrics without noting the jolt and charge with which they are delivered — it would be the equivalent of reading a script without seeing the images onscreen, or making a synopsis that doesn't acknowledge tone or mood.

Identifying the "meaning" of a track becomes even more difficult when it deals in conflicting associations of word and melody: if it pairs vanilla lyrics with a sleazy, lecherous bass, so that all the suggestiveness is in the sound itself. When music balances two sets of values, sonic and verbal, which comes out on top? The most intriguing approach a song can take is to be two-faced: to say one thing and do another.

To write off an artist on the basis of vapid lyrics is premature, at the least. The huge success and hypnotic effect of Rihanna's *Umbrella* (2007) has little to do with its banal verses, which ostensibly offer love and support, even though Rihanna's nonchalant voice plays against this. What makes the song haunting is the way the sound "ella" becomes peculiarly detached from the umbrella of the title; this tail-word is repeated again and again, like a little hook or uptick that floats off into its own chorus, independent of literal meaning. It could be an abstract sound or a bit of mispronounced Spanish, but there's much more energy in the "ella" than anything that precedes it, so that all the verses and half the chorus are merely the launchpad for this hook. The listener also registers the contradiction between the song's token message of caring and the smack-down of Rihanna's heavy butch voice ("eh, eh, eh"), which suggests indifference rather than empathy.

The duplicitous nature of pop makes it the ideal genre for communicating a range of viewpoints, without ever committing to a definite stance. This is especially effective when it comes to polarizing topics such as adultery, prostitution, and pick-ups — and, by extension, certain tempos, rhythms, and structures are intrinsically suited to these subjects. Delving into the surprisingly great history of prostitution in pop — Donna Summer's *Bad Girls* (1979), Randy Crawford's *Street Life* (1979), Blondie's *Call Me* (1980) — it becomes clear that songs about sex work benefit from a certain pace: a marching, authoritative beat that hooks you into walking the beat before you know it. There is an enduring ambiguity about these tracks: the lyrics of *Street Life* and *Bad Girls* refer to the disapproval and despair faced by prostitutes, but both songs are propelled by a relentless series of beats — like the click of spike heels — that convey the addictive sense of pounding the pavement.

In a similar vein, songs that deal with pimping have often played a double game of sternness and sexuality. In Bobby Womack's *Across 110th Street* (1972), the singer expresses some regret over "doing whatever I had to do to survive," but these doubts are pushed aside by the magnificent wave-like "oohs" that surge across the song, and the way the strings crest just as the pimp reveals he is "trying to catch a woman that's weak" — a motive that comes across as tragic rather than venal. *Pusherman* (1972) sees Curtis Mayfield as a criminal declaring his own villainy, yet those warnings pale against the step-like invitation of the descending bass and the complete seduction of Mayfield's voice, which swoops down and up, guiding us towards effortless highs.

A tune can be insidious or moralizing in itself, and therefore challenge the triteness of its words. Janet Jackson's astonishing *If* (1993) combines simplistic lyrics with a melody whose tone is somewhat less certain: it drifts underneath and changes form, charging unexpected words with power and muting others. The narrator begins in a low murmur, describing all the erotic gifts she would bestow on a man "if I was your girl," before stipulating loudly in the chorus that "I'm not, so I can't, and I won't." On paper, that decision seems steadfast, but listening to the record, the word "if" is dangled like a tantalizing feather, and all the coiled and compressed energy of the song lies in the mumbled verse rather than the chorus.

The greatest tracks don't have a point of view, as such; the most captivating music is slippery, telegraphing a secret meaning while asserting its intentions at face value. Even a hackneyed line can be a source of wonder if it is backed by fascinating rhythms. When a lyric is reduced to abstraction or becomes lost in the energy of a guitar, what matters is the grip of a voice matched with a particular note. In a way, music is the art that most readily confounds political readings, because a phrase is constantly heightened or undermined by the patterns that underlie it. Music affects by its implication of pauses and emphases: the emotionally descriptive prolonging that signals a view without stating it.

However, these kinds of effects are rarely discussed in music criticism. The long-line "ooh" that begins *Across 110th Street* is one of the most powerful sounds in contemporary music, yet it has received a fraction of the attention given to the lyrics of, say, Bob Dylan or Joni Mitchell; the latter rely on a conscious appreciation of language rather than a response to the irrational effects of music. Surely the "Oooohhh, baby" of R&B is as worthy of study as the elegant phrase of a Dylan – but where is the body of writing to prove it? The fine critic Marcello Carlin, known for his sound-by-sound analysis of tracks, is one of the few writers willing to get to the bottom of an "ooh, aah," but he is very much an exception.

The majority of reviews continue to follow the hierarchy set by Robert Christgau, the self-proclaimed dean of American rock critics who has, for 50 years, panned album after album of "fatuous" and "say-nothing" lyrics in favor of "verbally distinguished" work. For Christgau, Dylan is rock's greatest songwriter for the fact that he "drops wonderful lines galore," whereas the likes of Marvin Gaye and Phoebe Snow occasionally deliver "vapid" messages. Even Prince is guilty of "incoherent, or mushy," "poorly informed" lyrics — as if general knowledge was a prerequisite for pop! Carole King comes in for a measure of praise, despite not reaching the "bitter hard-rock perspicuity of Bob Dylan or Mick Jagger" which appears to be the gold standard of critical approval. However, Christgau cautions that King's real "talent is as a melodist," since some of her lyrics are "vapid and/or overblown." The fact that an artist's worth is qualified by saying she is "only" good at melody shows the assumptions at work here: that musical authority is spoken, and "personal" songwriting means lyrical ingenuity.

This tradition of thinking has been hard to escape. The overwhelming critical tendency is to review the stance suggested by the lyrics and the influences represented by the music, rather than listening intensely to a song and the individual moments of strangeness it brings. For British writer Neil Kulkarni, the problem with current music criticism is that reviewers are largely focused on "filing" music as if it were prose, driven by the urge to "place, contextualise, describe, commercially delineate ... simply *comprehending* music and never rhapsodizing."

An alternative approach would acknowledge that some of the greatest lyrics in the world are indeed vague rather than pithy: for instance, the cries of "Oh! Oh!" or "I know" or "Whoa, whoa" in the work of artists such as Bill Withers and Chaka Khan. In *Ain't No Sunshine* (1971), Withers breaks into a mesmerizing repetition of "I know, I know, I know..." that conveys a senseless desperation precisely because it's not conventionally articulate. We can never put a finger on what the narrator knows, and that's the point.

It may be the very absence of subject and coherence – that "say-nothing" quality – that makes a song beguiling. Like

Withers' "I know, I know...," the best lyrics can be driving, passionate, and yet elusive of meaning or motive. The basis for the Happy Mondays' finest track, *Loose Fit* (1990), is an obsessive repetition from which literal meaning has vanished: "Has to be a loose fit, has to be a loose fit... 'S gotta be a loose fit." The dawdling guitar rhythms create a feeling of idle disorientation, as the singer is on a quest to find something he can't name or picture. What he's seeking should not be too clear-cut: a "loose fit" is perfectly imprecise, a form that hangs off the frame just so. Through the haze of guitars, this demand makes itself known again and again, and the song takes its force from the abstract nature of this compulsion.

On Saint Etienne's mood-driven album *So Tough* (1993), one of the most minimal and arresting tracks is *Conchita Martinez*, presumably named for the strapping tennis player of the 1990s. Lyrically it contains only one line, one certainty ("Conchita, I know, I know it should have been Conchita"), but this conviction is repeated fervently, with a riff from Rush's *The Spirit of the Radio* (1980) spiraling underneath. This song is notable for the way it combines total urgency and specificity with zero back-story; it takes a heroic rock riff and turns it into a pulsing undercurrent, with only the thinnest of narrative pretexts, a girl named Conchita, to explain its intensity. The overall effect is one of mysterious fixation, and mystery is undervalued in pop these days: the beat or word that repeats for no reason, but remains uniquely compelling and ineradicable.

In the last few decades, some of the most extraordinary lines in popular music have been far from writerly: to take two disparate examples, Beyoncé's "Top, top, top, top, top!" and the immortal repetition of "Zoo-wa, zoo-wa, zoo-wa-la-la" in Deee-Lite's *Good Beat* (1990). The latter is a sublime instance of musical logic trumping rational sense: Deee-Lite gained international fame with their witty debut *Groove is in the Heart*, but it's on their third single, *Good Beat*, that they truly excite our responses to sound. Nothing could be more generic than the song's refrain of "I just wanna hear a good beat," but this throwaway lyric is just a placeholder before "knowing" sentences are cast aside and language falls to pieces. In the first half of the song, Lady Miss Kier sings "ooh-ooh-ooh, ah-ah-ah" in a slurred manner, alternating her cries with intelligible phrases. But eventually words melt off, the units of communication dissolve, and "ooh-ah" turns into "zoo-wa, zoo-wa," an ecstatic nonsense dialect that will carry us through the last minute of the track. Just as the "ella" of Rihanna's *Umbrella* becomes unhooked, language is denatured until it becomes nothing more than an automatic mouth movement.

Beyoncé's *Love on Top* (2011) is a song made memorable by the idiosyncrasies of a voice. This track is the highlight of the singer's fourth album, but it has been overlooked in comparison to her other hits. Critically it has been judged a minor work, a mere throwback to the pop euphoria of the 1980s – as if paradise grows on trees, or melodic pleasure can be had on demand. The utter exuberance of this song is no small achievement, and part of it stems from Beyoncé's fascination with the word "top." The narrator of *Love on Top* reveals that her boyfriend has, after some struggle, decided to prioritize her needs above everyone else's. Success is celebrated, with the caveat that perhaps it needn't have taken so long. These complications mean that the song's jubilation is earned, rather than a given, and when we get to the peak of the chorus, she exclaims, "Top, top, top, top, top!" Beyoncé taps the word "top" everywhere, on notes high and low, as if banging a gong she can never get tired of, and her tone is emotionally specific: gleeful and a little smug.

The singer concedes that "nothing's perfect," but for now, shaking this shiny new rattle is all she wants to do, and happiness is represented by the word "top," which changes key, escalating higher and higher. As the critic Ricky Schweitzer puts it, "it is energy and not ego that drives the constantly rising progression." Beyoncé's singing has a strident oomph, a ticking impatience unusual in a love song; each time she sings "Come on baby, it's you," she gives her voice a compulsive little squeeze and clenches her fist, before kicking up the chorus and changing keys once again. When she reaches the word "top," the backing vocals ("tup, tup, tup") sound like tiny sipping noises, partaking of the cup. *Love on Top* shows that, with creative interpretation, a miraculous emotional range can be achieved with unremarkable lyrics and a conventional uplift. The words appear to be chosen, not for their novelty or variety, but for the effect they have on the mouth and voice. Singing "from ear to ear" involuntarily draws the lips into a smile, as does saying "hear" and "near," while "top" is perfect for shaping the mouth into a smirk.

This is yet another factor that needs to be considered when analyzing lyrics: the fact that words may only be a pretext to stretch the lips in a particular way, so as to give special resonance to the voice. Think of the Frankie Valli theme from *Grease* (1978), written by Barry Gibb, and the way it forces you to perform its own echo ("Grease is the word, is the word, that you heard..."), pursing the mouth and funneling the voice that comes out of it. With "word" and "heard," we curve our lips and repeatedly hone the sound, until it acquires a sheen. If the mouth can be persuaded to take up certain shapes, then our attitude towards a song is formed before we are aware of its lyrical content: some words require an open, vulnerable mouth, while others compel closure. This kind of effect means that stock phrases may not be as straightforward as they seem, and it makes it problematic to reject lyrics on the grounds of being stale or common. In any case, originality has little to do with how easily words are internalized: a clichéd line may roll off the tongue, but the odd title of The Gap Band's *Oops Up Side Your Head* (1979) fits just as neatly into the mouth, popping like a grape into its oval shape.

A great song should work on our instincts first: we should feel the pleasure of pouting or smoothly extruding words before we have time to digest what we're saying. In other words, the mouth needs to be transfixed before the mind. Unfortunately, the reverse seems to happen with most acclaimed music today. Personally, I rarely respond to lyrics that scan very easily independent of tone and melody, which is the case with balladeers such as Nick Cave and Leonard Cohen. The works of these songwriters tend to be structured by predictable poetic meters, with the strokes between stanzas all too clear to the ear. Their obvious sophistication is an appeal to the conscious brain, encouraging an appreciation of craft and intelligence, rather than a spontaneous impulse that seizes the mouth and the hips. Nothing escapes the dry voice and fine mind of the speaker.

The most exciting moments in popular music don't rely on literary cachet: certainly, quoting phrases doesn't do them justice. In many Stevie Wonder songs, the phonetic impact of words takes precedence over their strict usage: *Uptight* (1966) is sung by a young man who has attained glamour despite his poverty and poor clothes. Although he only has one shirt and a suit that's out of style, he struts confidently into the night: he's feeling "uptight, clean out of sight." The word "uptight" here does not suggest prissy or proper; if anything, the meaning is closer to "upright," as in a zipped-up, streamlined air of chic. The title makes no literal sense at all, but it is absolutely the right word for the feeling that the song means to transmit. The narrator wears an unfashionable suit, but to him it feels smart and bolt upright, like a snappable second skin. "Uptight" gives a sense of being sleek and wrapped-up like no other word could, especially since it matches the song's context of an improvised piece tossed on at the last moment. Literal accuracy is not a problem here, since lyrics must be judged by different rules than those of prose: it is not as if a wide vocabulary, grammatical correctness, and consistent use of metaphor are the most important factors in songwriting.

In fact, songs often benefit from expressions that are technically wrong but uncannily apt. The Doors' *L.A. Woman* (1971) is sung by a flaky man who has just arrived in Hollywood, with the ideal of a California babe in mind. To this generic image of woman, he insists: "If they say I never loved you, then you know they are a liar." It is a bizarre choice of words, but in this trippy song where every other line is sung distractedly, the suspension of grammatical rules seems right. "You know that they are liars" would seem too formal and compressed, but "you know they are a liar" allows the right amount of distance between the singer and the point of view he lazily dangles towards us. Naturally, we also think back to the last time Jim Morrison was suspected of being a liar: when he sang of the funeral pyre in *Light My Fire* (1967). Context is everything here: we have to look at how a phrase operates within a song and an artist's oeuvre, rather than independently on the page.

This is not to deny the value of ingenious wordplay. Listen to *Shake Your Head (Let's Go to Bed)* (1992), that sublime, underrated single by Was (Not Was), featuring the unlikely vocal duo of Ozzy Osbourne and Kim Basinger. The two recite a series of inspired proverbs in which good intentions and brains come to nothing in the face of stark reality ("You can't read a robot's mind," "You can't purify bad blood"). Instead of angst, the lyrics advocate a return to simple-minded hedonism ("You can't influence the masses … let's go to bed.") But this sunny, apolitical attitude is expressed by sounds as much as words: the heavy vocal processing, tacky synthesizer and house beat transmit blissed-out impersonality.

As the band's name usefully indicates, Was (Not Was) are dedicated to the principles of rhythm rather than logic or syntax, and this song is a wonderful hymn to the pleasures of anesthesia, in which desensitization is conveyed musically, without resorting to a term like "comfortably numb." Rather than writing over-determined lyrics, what the band has found is a satirical *sound* that evokes the feeling of being tranquil and light-headed. The glitzy production and nagging noise of the synth conjure a superficial world much more effectively than any verbal account. David Was' lyrics describing the failures of rationality are delicious on paper, but being accompanied by the "mindless" stomp of the beat takes them to another level. We are not told that numbness and nullity are perversely sexy; instead, we get to sensuously absorb these values from the record.

Which is more complex: to have a single, eloquent narrator rail against the ills of society, or to produce a voice and sound that give off contrasting associations? More than twenty years later, *Shake Your Head* is still an enigma, thanks to its self-righteous narration undermined by shrill, offbeat noises. While the lyrics question materialist values, this mix has all the hallmarks of a glossy house production. Instead of showing obvious cynicism, Was (Not Was) enact and perform different versions of irony, resulting in a track of mixed moods: shrewd and loony, aloof and lascivious. A range of vivid personalities is packed into this song: Basinger alternates between severity and an orgasmic "ooh," while Osbourne's whacked-out vocals combine stoner, trained ape, and the voice of doom.

The above might seem like a put-down of smart, literate songwriting, but there are many word-obsessed singers who have managed to find musical equivalents for their verbosity. Morrissey and Pavement's Stephen Malkmus are two brilliant author-musicians whose songs parody their own didactic nature. Malkmus deliberately struggles to graft rambling sentences onto hummable tunes, painfully enunciating each syllable and sometimes cutting off the ends to fit the rhyme. Morrissey makes language come alive with his slashing punctuation and dead-on caricatures of English manners. His songs mourn his own fatally articulate nature as a songwriter, who can never resist jamming in more words than necessary. In *The More You Ignore Me, The Closer I Get* (1994), he plays the part of an insistent stalker who can't stop talking, and ridiculously lengthens one verse by piling on metaphors ("I bear more grudges, than lonely high court judges / When you sleep, I will creep into your thoughts / Like a bad debt, that you can't pay, take the easy way.") As he draws out the sentence, his cadence becomes ever grander and his voice more fluted and regal: it's a marvelous deflation of pomposity.

Best of all, there is Edwyn Collins' great *A Girl Like You* (1995), a song that is happy to deal in lyrical platitudes for the most part, saving itself for an incongruously wordy section towards the end ("I hope to God I'm talkin' metaphorically / Hope that I'm talkin' allegorically"). Having written a sure-fire hit with an irresistible chorus ("I've never met a girl like you before"), Collins parodies the yearning for artistic credibility by shoving a token bit of erudition into a love song. But the bold gesture of rhyming "metaphorically" with "allegorically" occurs just before the return of that catchy chorus, and the violence of the diatribe is lost as the song falls back into its boppy 1960s rhythms. For gifted wordsmiths such as Collins, Malkmus, and Morrissey, musical success lies in making the love of language strange. The sculpting of phrases is seen as a curious, decadent habit: a personal predilection rather than a flaunting of one's intellect or catering to a highbrow audience.

Adopting a knowing, sophisticated tone may be one way to ensure decent reviews for an album (or a book or film, for that matter), but it is an approach that excludes mystery. It is the sense of an "unknowing" voice that gives music its exceptional power, the perception of elements that hover at the limits of the author's control. Jay-Z's most intriguing attribute is not his super-tight, concise rapping. It is the way that, when performing live, his strong, singular persona will bleed into other characters. After a virtuosic demonstration of flow, Jay-Z occasionally descends into dreamy, "silly" states by uttering a falsetto shriek, or slipping into a fastidious voice not quite his own. These little digressions – often marked by the strange mincing enunciation of a word – are part of what make Jay-Z compelling as an artist, taking him beyond flawless execution.

Even the voice of Kylie Minogue, which is not conventionally "good," leaves us with a metallic tang and sourness that comes from being slightly off-key. The faults and cracks in her vocals are what make them recognizable. Minogue's voice may not be endlessly elastic, but I don't think her hits would be as effective coming from a singer with rich tone and a superb range – the songs might even seem meaningless. It's probably no coincidence that her best tracks (*Better the Devil You Know* and *Step Back in Time*, 1990, *Never Too Late,* 1989) have a feeling of shrugging and approximation: life's not perfect, but so what? *Better the Devil You Know* is a favorite of Nick Cave's, with its impassive depiction of a misused woman coming back for more, and Minogue's flip delivery is what drives the point home: the singer's nonchalance in the face of cruel treatment.

Two of her more recent singles, *Can't Get You Out of My Head* (2001) and *Chocolate* (2004), have the air of annoyingly persistent jingles, and they flaunt it happily. The gorgeous *Chocolate* is full of musical and verbal references to lushness and smoothness ("slowly melt me down"), picturing desire as a Cadbury-like swirl. *Confide in Me* (1994) is one of

Minogue's rare critical successes in that it foregrounds its own disposability, the video envisioning Minogue as a phone-sex worker who fakes being cute and girlie. Again, these last three songs wouldn't work with sensuous vocals: what's required is a voice with a shiny cheap patina that aggressively "sells" the chorus. When the *Guardian*'s Alexis Petridis criticizes Minogue's work as "glossy, depthless pop" with "excruciating lyrics," all one can say is: right on target. Music is not always about depth and timbre: sometimes a song is best served by a slick, offhand treatment.

So there are other kinds of love. The classical ballad extols romantic and erotic passion, but pop was designed for other purposes: unnatural fondness, foolish crushes, love for sale. Reviews will always praise artists who demonstrate coherent intelligence, yet pop's distinction lies in its ability to shuck off sensible opinions.

The capacity for non-verbal utterances to conjure specific images is part of the magic of pop music, in that it appears to defy reason. But common sense and taste have no place in pop: the biggest challenge for a songwriter is to work with these involuntary and immediate associations in the heat of the moment, whatever their source. Snazzy poetic lines look great on the page, but they can come across as stilted when sung. What's required is an extra animation guided by intuition: the precise emphasis given to the "ooh."

If there is one word, one sound, I could retain from the history of popular music, it would be the monumental up-up-up breath of Chaka Khan. You know the one: the escalating "Oh-oh-oh-ohhh" that triggers the chorus in *Ain't Nobody* (1983). This sublime, full-body exhalation is, for my money, the most expressive sound in pop. We build up to it via a tense undercurrent of bass, so that Khan's outburst comes as a supremely satisfying climax. I would happily live in that sound forever – it is endlessly invigorating and produces the rapture of being high on helium. But Khan's is only one in a canon of "ohs" and "oohs" that give outrageous pleasure in pop. There is the hoot that crowns almost every disco anthem, a salacious catcall best used in Michael Zager Band's *Let's All Chant* (1977). There is the flexible, swoosh-like "ooh" that makes The Chimes' Pauline Henry one of the great, underused soul voices. Most enduringly, we have the double cry that kicks off Rob Base & DJ E-Z Rock's *It Takes Two* (1988): a sample that has appeared in literally thousands of dance tracks with no loss of power. These two cries are difficult to place, yet instantly evocative: the first one sounds like a screech of alarm, while the second is more of an affirmative shout-out. It's a call-and-response that is not quite human, not quite hyena: a scratch that never fails to mark the surface of our awareness.

One could write the story of American contemporary music based largely on a history of "oohs": their nature and variety, their context and delivery (see the Appendix for a countdown of the most memorable). In particular, funk and R&B are founded on the power and seductiveness of non-verbal sounds. Lyric quotes can't contain the shape-shifting nature of this music, in which every yelp or bark alters a song's feel. Pop is a medium for immediacy rather than erudition, and "ooh" tends to be the moment where a song crystallizes its emotional affect. On TLC's debut album *Oooooohhh... On the TLC Tip* (1992), the female R&B group issue the title cry in a hundred different ways: as a nuanced utterance full of longing, as the parody of a clucking boyfriend, and as a way to mock girlish helplessness.

"Ooh" is the sound that propels Quiet Storm, the highly influential genre of smooth, late-night soul pioneered by African American artists since the 1970s. At first glance, the lyrics of these songs may seem pedestrian, but just listen to the dynamics of the music. Regina Belle's classic *Baby Come to Me* (1989) contains the familiar imagery of heart-piercing and spine-tingling love, and the track starts off in a routine manner, with Belle declaring her passion in clear, beautiful tones. But there comes a point in the chorus where her voice becomes fudged and thickened with desire; her speech grows slurred as she mutters something about "got it goin' on, you're turnin' me on." There is a strong sense of eros in the way that the singer uses her lips to smear and muddy the lyrics. The song comes alive during these "oh" moments, when inarticulate longing distorts the mouth and confuses the words; Belle is able to narrow and expand the timbre of her voice, like a ribbon that twists and unfurls.

A great, self-reflexive track on the significance of "oh" is *Motownphilly* (1991), the debut single of critically scorned quartet Boyz II Men. For this groundbreaking work alone, the band atones for their subsequent ballads and earns their place in pop heaven. The song lyrically references the evolution of music, from 1960s Motown to 1970s Philly soul to hip-hop. As they describe their history, they perform it orally, quoting the "daa-da, daa-da" of their school years in South Street. Since the story must be related in musical terms, a rap interlude gives way to the guys singing a clip from their first audition: a further series of "daa-das," this time ending in a long, sensual groan: "Oh-oh-ohhh." With that last sound, the band doesn't need to say anything more about their origins: that "ohhh" is the deep cathartic sigh of Philadelphia soul. Subtle variations on "oh" and "daa-da" mark the changes in music as it takes a geographically specific route around the country.

There is the convincing belief that the inflection of a note can tell you everything you need to know about a region. These are localized sounds that impart specific moods to music: "oh" is the unit in a system of values that is sonically rather than lyrically based. Through their cries, the singers choose to flaunt their harmony and smoothness rather than their virility, and that keys us into their aspirations and backgrounds. In bringing several schools of sound together, Boyz II Men present themselves as a long-awaited fusion of genres and voices, culminating in the sound of "oh." *Motownphilly* is in itself a document of the times; tracking the boys on their journey to a global audience, with each bridge taking us back musically to their hometown of Philadelphia.

Ecstatic moments like these are more likely to be found in hip-hop, R&B, and commercial pop than in guitar rock or any of the more respectable genres, since the author who holds forth from his or her instrument tends to do so from the perspective of a single mind rather than an odd convergence of voices and sounds. I propose that some of the most stimulating work of the last thirty years has been created by maximalist, mercurial artists such as Janet Jackson, TLC, and the maverick rapper Neneh Cherry — three of the artists prominently featured in this book. Instead of warm organic tones and conventional refinement, what these acts offer are disturbing noises and synthetic textures, which are simultaneously addictive and puzzling. Identifying the ways and means of this music involves getting past the conventions of language as we know it: for instance, exploring how a word becomes weirdly de-emphasized when matched with a certain beat.

Most of all, it means moving beyond the masterly tradition of songwriting to revel in the greatest sounds ever released: the exact propulsion and energy of Janet Jackson's "ooh-ooh-ooh, yeah," the vibrating "whoa, whoa" of Chaka Khan, and the enchanted "ella" of Rihanna's *Umbrella*. One of the songs of the century, *Umbrella* may as well be titled "Waiting for Ella," since we spend the verses waiting for the curiosity of that smooth, well-turned sound: "ella, ella," which repeats like a curve before flattening into "eh, eh." The secret of pop is the mystery of "ella" and "eh": little arcs of sound left to hang out, like the irresistible hooks that they are.

MALICIOUS POP:
THE CUTTING SOUNDS OF NENEH CHERRY

When the video for *Buffalo Stance* first appeared in 1988, it seemed raw and almost ugly, with its harsh noise set against yellow and purple psychedelia. The artist herself, Neneh Cherry, was equally anomalous. Here was a singer with a vaguely New York drawl and the odd Cockney riff, who seemed unplaceable in terms of character as well as nationality. She scowled as she rapped, her juicy foul mouth pressed close to the camera. According to the lyrics, the object of her scorn was a pimp who had tried to recruit her. Yet Cherry was just as dismissive of everyone else on the street: the "nasty" girls with permed hair, the weak-willed boys who came running when called. The cacophonous mix of samples and tribal beats suggested a portrait of street life, with an unforgiving narrator breaking the scene down to its tawdriest details.

Even today, Cherry remains one of the most disorientingly eclectic of artists. On her debut album, *Raw Like Sushi* (1989), most of the tracks are catchy yet confusingly dense, throwing us off with their mood changes and far-flung references. Her voice switches nationalities within a single breath; she can come across as a sage or a brat, sophisticated or cacklingly malicious. Her tough persona implies a straightforward approach to her craft, but what the music presents is harder to decipher.

On the first track, *Buffalo Stance*, Cherry already comes across as a fully formed artist: powerful and casually multicultural, as we might expect from an African-Swedish singer raised in Yorkshire and Long Island. But Cherry is no "minority" demanding to be empowered: this is a performer who originates a new sound without asking for permission. Her voice immediately assumes a central position; there's no sense of her breaking through from the margins. Her first act as leader is to call out the members of her team: first, the hi-hat, then the tambourine, and finally the DJ and his records. It's as if, before the track can begin, each circle has to be set spinning within the Cherry universe, and she is in a position to control all of them.

When we get to the critique of the pimp and the girls, Cherry's voice is superior and strident; throughout the album, there tends to be a view of boys as dominated and unripe, while the girls are predatory, standing around "wearing padded bras, sucking beer through straws." Men may be limp, but these young women are even less sensual, with their lacquered lips pursed over a can. So this first part of the song is rather abject, with its hawking voice, and its allusions to gross female display.

But *Buffalo Stance* is a song of many moods, as Cherry goes on to alternate between anger and softness, anti-materialism, and a high fashion attitude. A rising synth figure bubbles us up to a heavenly chorus ("No money man can win my love / It's sweetness that I'm thinking of ... I'll give you love baby, not romance") that shows a rare tenderness in the narrator. Even though the track has been unrelenting up to now, the bubbling and the melody expose an underlying effervescence.

We don't get to coast on this feeling for long; the second time the chorus appears, Cherry re-armors herself and reveals that she is not alone: instead, she is part of a hip fashion elite (Cherry and producer Cameron McVey met as models in London, after all). Despite the romantic message of the chorus, the Buffalo are a catwalk crew, for whom glamour comes first ("Looking good when it comes to the crunch / Looking good's a state of mind"). To emphasize the point, Cherry seizes and recharges the end of the phrase, shouting fiercely, "State of mind, don't look behind you! / State of mind or you'll be dead!" This creates a feeling of whiplash, as if the line has been picked up and thrashed loose.

Abrasive effects like these define the song, as well as the album. Cherry and McVey's style is not the warm, full-bodied sound of R&B: it has a much more inorganic feel, favoring fizzy noise over the deep tones of funk or soul. "Buffalo Stance" has a coiled, compressed sound; beats form little eddies and bubbles that correspond to the blooming digital shapes of the video. The synth is thin and airy, evoking something crude and mass-produced: that's what makes the track distinctive rather than generically tasteful. Audiences may expect great music to be rich and rootsy; *Raw Like Sushi* remains strange because its sound is exactly the opposite — bright, sharp, and cold, a rejection of the past.

The album's second track, *Manchild*, also seems curiously mechanical at first. The title character is a guy with a run-down car, a cheating girlfriend, and no willpower, so it's not surprising that we get a hypnotic sense of draining away. The strings have a repetitive, droning sound; they move gradually up or down a tone, so that the entire song seems to be slipping down a slope. A program of beats forms a continually revolving and reversing pattern, and the track feels as if it's shuffling or rotating by degrees (the video ingeniously matched this idea of constant slippage by showing Cherry surrounded by tilting levels of water.) However, what's elating is the way that the song repeatedly threatens to lose its motor — and then regains it, by a whisker. All that downward movement should lead to a dead end, but just before momentum runs out, the vocal lifts to even out and stabilize the track. The lyrics are self-reflexive; the phrase "Turn around, ask yourself" is used as a pivot, a chance for the song to do a 180-degree turn.

In terms of rhythmic structure and surprises, *Manchild* may be even more of a feat than *Buffalo Stance*; it is astonishing in its intricate raps that upend themselves midway. Cherry plays with syncopation, sometimes teasing out words or topping a dense phrase with light notes. The track ends unexpectedly, when all instrumentation vanishes, leaving a single phrase in the foreground; the final words we hear are "'Cause I believe in miracles and words in heavy doses." That last line really is a concentrated dose, as a continuously chugging rap suddenly stops, revealing that the whole song is a closed circuit.

The next two tracks are more conventionally melodic, yet both contain sublime moments in which sonic effects absolutely coincide with the subject of the lyrics. *Kisses on the Wind* is a paean to a girl whose breeziness enchants the young neighborhood boys. Her presence is reflected in the salsa rhythm, Spanish dialogue, and the song's flowing feel. The melody keeps billowing upwards ("More like a woman, she walks like one") and is thus subtly suggestive of the female shape. *Inna City Mamma* is unusual for Cherry in that it sticks to one city and one genre: NYC blues. What makes this particular take compelling is the way that the instrumentation works with the theme of masochism: the bassline keeps coming back for an extra note, while the drums return to give one last tap. It is as if the narrator is attempting to close the book on a subject, but she can't leave well enough alone, and the song trails into a smoky finish.

As the fog from the last track clears, what emerges is the beginnings of *The Next Generation*: perhaps the most puzzling and original Cherry song, full of spite, vigor, and low-life humor. This is a bawd's song, in which Cherry performs multiple characters: a bully who comes with her own cheer squad, a sarcastic girl who calls you "honey," and a mother whose lap is open to all children. As the sounds of birds flutter past, there is the sensation of a vibrant, open market, but it soon becomes ominously clear that this is actually a black market, a baby market. Fertility has turned to rampant breeding — of the rank, putrid kind. Japanese, German, and French phrases open the song, and although there are no ethnic slurs, a kind of leering potential for racism is present.

The "sensible" Cherry persona is sickened by the thought of a baby wrangler, but her voice then takes on the personality of the peddler, salivating over provocative racial combos ("Black babies, white babies / Quarter Puerto Rican, two sixths Chinese / Any combination you could possibly imagine"). In this new world, she envisions babies and their ethnicities being divvied out according to value. Cherry's maternal character is disapproving, but the bawd can't resist a dig at this epidemic; she reacts with gasps of shock and faux-delight. She has a coarse, derisive laugh that the song then turns into a sample, unsettling us further.

Overall, *The Next Generation* is a celebration of birth, creativity, and fecundity, but as Cherry knows, a song about the miracle of life would make for a pretty boring cut. So she goes into the most squalid aspects of procreation: the filth of reproduction, a world of diapers and diseases. "Push-push-push" shows that the whole impetus of the song is the birth movement: the pressure of the sex act and the mother's motion in expelling new life. The song builds a joyous cycle out of all these noises and gestures, backed by a panorama of free jazz and zoological sounds. We can picture the song's setting as an arena, in which vivid characters whirl around while Cherry sits as the earth mother, bouncing a baby on her lap.

Still, this loosely connected jig requires some sort of ending. Will the song finish on a humanist note, or will it trail off to imply endless procreation? Nothing so predictable. Towards the end, a drumline has the effect of lifting Cherry to the podium, where she asks us, "Ain't that right?" At that, the sound immediately reduces to one beat, skating off and skipping back before Cherry laughs and says confidently, "Right." The rhythm doesn't resolve or repeat; all sounds bounce back to the singular voice at the mic.

And that's the substance of the album: five extraordinary tracks, several intriguing numbers (*Heart*, *So Here I Come*), and a couple of middling ones (*Love Ghetto*, *Outré Risqué Locomotive*) that prefigure Cherry's next two albums, *Homebrew* (1992) and *Man* (1996), in that they are much more homogenous, rooted in a single mood and identity. Cherry is at her best when her persona seems conflicted, dividing into multiple voices and moving through different tones with exhilarating speed.

Although she clearly draws from a wealth of cultural influences, Neneh Cherry has never been anything so wholesome as a "world" artist. Released at a time when both hip-hop and sushi were considered alternative, this album still stuns with its unique take on rawness: not the fuzzy lo-fi kind, but a sound that is actually grating and alarming to the ear. *Raw Like Sushi* is proof that great albums don't have to take on heroic structures; the record's most distinguishing feature is its exploration of superficiality and tackiness on both sonic and verbal levels. Instead of a sense of grandeur or orchestration, transcendence is achieved through an accumulation of small details: a sampled screech, the odd tinny note, an image of tiny-mouthed women sucking through straws. Soulful phrases are combined with synthetic textures, so that each sound retains its own idiosyncrasy, rather than being refined into a whole.

The Next Generation might be the ultimate Cherry creation in that it manages to fire up so many contradictions:

the life process and decaying sexuality, inclusiveness and bigotry, a huge song cycle made up of chaotic, individual sounds. In this track, above all others, she proves herself an artist with the courage to bypass notions of taste and cohesion. Balanced with an epic vision of the future is an appreciation for the cheap, the sordid, and the perverse: these are the kinds of contrasts only Cherry can keep in play.

JANET JACKSON'S SCHOOL OF ROCK

Janet has a torn, raw, "wet" voice — ideal for expressing the wariness of an outsider, as well as the sexual urgency of her later albums. Over the years it has been criticized for its lack of power and projection, but that asphyxiated gasp gives the necessary stress to anthems such as *What Have You Done for Me Lately* (1986), her voice itself jerking and enforcing a mode of discipline. Conversely, in what Jackson refers to as her "baby-making" tracks, the choked voice creates a sense of edge and vulnerability, the equivalent of saying "these words catch in my throat." Breathlessness has many meanings in Jackson: the nervy girl holding her ground in the face of catcalls, the excitement of the desiring woman, the courtesan putting on a show. With her longtime producers Jimmy Jam and Terry Lewis, Jackson has developed a range of characters uniquely suited to her timbre. The absence of vocal pyrotechnics puts all the focus on texture, the twists of the velvet rope. Janet has the ability to change from taut and guarded to supple without noticeably shifting her tone. She is one of the few artists who can make being armored seem sexy, eroticizing both control and its loss.

That tension between angularity and sensuality has always marked the singer's best work: the greatness of her songs is in their variation between strictness and sweet relief, a dynamic that restrains then releases our bodies. With its daringly suppressed verses and break-through chorus, *If* (1992) is the culmination of Jackson's work with Jam and Lewis. It is a rock song that packs in a ridiculous amount of intensity, all for the sake of a brief — and ecstatic — reprieve. The opening sounds like the start-up of some huge machine: a searing guitar and the chug of bow on strings suggest the grinding of gears. Once warmed up, we prepare for a surge of energy, but the song wrong-foots us by heading down into Janet's vocal line, a near-monotone. These verses are weirdly muttered and compressed: almost unintelligible, with the odd high note or bright word ("body," "thighs") flashing above the detail. During the flashes, the melody jolts to life before being forced back down and controlled, like a flatline graph with sudden spikes. There is a narrative reason for all this constraint: the singer is flirting with an unavailable man. Flirting will only go far, but she'll show him a few highlights of what he's missing, including subliminal images of sex. Pressure builds and builds until the whole structure gives way, flowing into the bridge and the chorus.

After the tiny intervals and intricacy of the verse, the chorus comes across as epic and sweeping, with its plunging melody and full declarations ("If I was your girl, oh the things I'd do to you / I'd make you call out my name"). But all this big talk could end in nothing; everything still hinges on the title clause. The chorus ends with three defiant swipes ("But I'm *not*, so I *can't*, and I *won't*") before the low mumbling of the verse resumes, this time reducing down to pure beat ("down da down down down da down down").

Has any pop song gotten so much mileage out of a monotone? *If* races and throbs with variations on a single note before giving way to the highs of the chorus, elating in its sudden move from minimal to maximalist. Bernard Herrmann's theme for *North by Northwest* (1959) was powered by this sort of contrast: little hammering notes followed by incongruously large jumps, almost comic in the pairing of pedantry with daredevil acts. In music, taking meticulous steps before a headlong leap practically guarantees joy, but rarely has the process been so exaggerated. *If* inches forward in small increments: the lyrics are stifled, with only flickers of meaning (basically snapshots of flesh) emerging. In the last line of the verse, bottleneck tension bursts through, words accelerating towards the bridge. Cue exuberant release and passion — until the dread words "But if I was your girl," at which point, the fantasy snaps off and the genie goes back in the bottle.

If this song is about making us wait on desire — as the object of Janet's affections must wait — then the Brothers in Rhythm mix of *If* is even more effective at drawing out the anticipation. Their cut doubles the song's length and holds off the catharsis until close to the end, placing it behind sheets of ice. This remix lets us feel the oppositions within the Jackson persona: hot and cold, hard and yielding. The guitar opening of the original version is replaced with a cool catwalk stride:[1] bar after bar of trim, clipping beats that evoke glass panels sliding back and forth, separating us from what we long to hear. As a house act, Brothers in Rhythm show allegiance mainly to the beat, doling out snippets of the original tune – sometimes playing a little phrase that alludes to the bridge, but keeping back the euphoria of the top notes for later. We press our ear against this closed surface, listening for a break.

After several minutes of high-fashion strutting, the panels part and we get a longer dose of *If*: two airings of verse and chorus before it gets locked down again, iced over with layers of beats. The striding then restarts, going through a dozen iterations, some sampling the singer's own voice ("down, down, down") as an impatient, ticking

---

1 That a sound can be automatically read as "high-end" and exclusive shows that music has specific connotations that tend to bypass conventional analysis. If a track deals in a mixture of high-end and low-rent sounds, then our attention may be focused on this system of values rather than the lyrics.

counter. Glossy and impenetrable, this section tests our endurance — but when fulfillment does come, we're so glad we waited. The sweetness we taste when Janet's confession finally breaks through ("I've laid in bed excited over you / One hundred different ways I've gotten") is immensely satisfying, like biting through the frozen skin of a fruit — all the more rewarding for following a drought.

However, before it ends, the song has one more game of withdrawal to play. The original version of *If* concludes with a refusal ("If I was your woman, the things I'd do to you / But I'm *not*"), indicating that the entire song is one long conditional phrase, ready to be retracted on a whim. The Brothers in Rhythm communicate something similar, but musically. Although it begins austerely, their version gradually lays on all the trimmings, using a piano flourish to crown certain moments — before snatching up every effect and leaving us alone with that piano. So many pop remixes are about withholding — saving the fulfillment you know is coming, then giving it when you least expect it, all in a rush. This mix ends on a note of desertion — the capricious removal of a rhythm that has addicted one's body, put us through its paces. The song's theatrical machinery — the deluxe beats, horn samples, the whole architecture — can be whisked away without a trace, in line with the singer's all-or-nothing demands. The effect is of opening Pandora's box and then snapping it shut, leaving the listener to deal with the withdrawal from sound, the images that can't be unseen.

Jackson's first album with Jam and Lewis, the groundbreaking *Control* (1986), made it clear that her music was all about establishing parameters: of space, behavior, even of what her audience might be allowed to imagine. The title track begins with the manifesto "This is a story about control / My control / Control of what I say / Control of what I do," but it may as well be about control of what *you* do, given the hard-edged synth that nearly commands us to fall into line. The opening beat of *What Have You Done for Me Lately* is a ticking explosive, counting down to a reckoning with the singer's boyfriend; if this song's Janet is tightly wound, then her partner has been overly slack. Three of the album's love songs (*Let's Wait Awhile*, *Funny How Time Flies When You're Having Fun*, *You Can Be Mine*) express pleasure while keeping the listener in step and on track. In the prelude to a relationship, the singer insists on staying on her own timeline, controlling the pace of action.

At the time, Jackson's dance moves were linear and cautiously self-protective — marking territory before moving forward, defining the planes of her face, directing her hands to armor the body. Similarly, the structure of the songs puts you on notice: straightens your back, pulls you up, teaches you respect. The most enduring singles of this era (such as *Nasty*, *What Have You Done for Me Lately*, *The Pleasure Principle*, and from the next album, *Miss You Much*) are about staccato and discipline, administering authority through fiercely jagged rhythms. What's surprising is that the lesson never gets old: today, each of these songs still strikes freshly; the grooves they teach are utterly compelling to the body. We learn the importance of maintaining a line through the formalism of dance. The beats suspend your arms, poised to lash or defend, while locking the knees in an alert stance. *Miss You Much* (1989) and *What Have You Done for Me Lately* both contain passages of "down time" where the armor drops: in these confessional moments, a relaxed sensuality comes through and softens before we stand back to attention. *Nasty* (1986) doesn't have such an obvious relief period but, in taking the whip to the "nasty boys" of the neighborhood, the singer does make time for humor and even emotional nakedness ("I'm not a prude, I just want some self-respect"). That intelligence and flexibility within control ensures that these "strict" songs never become parodies of themselves.

I am still taken aback by the nerve of *Nasty*'s proposition: its image of a teenage Jackson walking into a den of wolves and sizing up each type. She is not scared, angry or vengeful — just possessed of an extraordinary lucidity that claims to see into the minds and bodies of lechers (at the cellular level, they are made up of nothing but "nasty food"). Calmly, she peels back every defense to reveal gross chomping, ugly ways of thinking — a pack of horndogs with slovenly mouths, harboring nasty fantasies about girls. There is such power in the singer's perspective: the way that she coolly diagnoses pathology, repulsed rather than threatened. She is not implicated in the abuse she receives: her gaze is solely directed outward, towards the offender. In the age of Internet trolls, this remains a remarkable model for turning "nasty" on its head. One is reminded of the words of Canadian activist Nellie McClung as she campaigned for voting rights: "Never explain, never retract, never apologize. Just get the thing done and let them howl!" In Jackson's case, hearing the wolves howl may even be part of the fun — she murmurs "I love this part" before reciting her list of charges.

The reason why this approach is so effective is that it is backed up musically on every level: by the strong, implacable chords that suggest firmly planted feet; by the steadiness and finality of the beats. The song's goal seems to be to define territory: to achieve harmonic stability and then vamp effortlessly around it. Janet is intense but sweatless, as evidenced by the tossed-off "don't mean a thing" and the synth phrase that comes after it. This insouciant little phrase is like a figure executing a neat spin and then walking off — it ends on an uptick, just before the line "all you nasty boys." Rhythmically, it's the equivalent of a cold shoulder brush-off — the dazzling power play followed by a clean exit. On this album, Janet is accusatory but ultimately cool, not risking burnout through anger.

Similarly, in *What Have You Done for Me Lately*, the singer describes problems with her deadbeat boyfriend, but nothing expresses pent-up angst more than the "ooh-ooh-ooh, yeah!" of the chorus. In the video, Janet pumps her shoulders while thinking over grievances, and resentment mounts during the verse. The specific push and release of the "ooh-ooh-ooh, yeah" is what stops the song from overheating — a way to let off steam without making any verbal concessions. One of the most mysterious aspects of pop is the way that non-verbal sounds can take on such precise emotional meaning, as if a feeling is determined to communicate itself without being named. Like the synth figure denoting the kiss-off in *Nasty*, the chorus of *What Have You Done for Me Lately* depends on a pattern of propulsion and retraction: an exact number of driving "oohs" before the slight relenting of the "yeah." In addition, the repetition of the minor third throughout the song keeps jabbing at the nerves, creating a sense of extreme angularity. Jam and Lewis are fond of chords that produce or aggravate tension — in this case, using narrow intervals to imply contracting space, backing the listener into a corner.

Although several of Jackson's hits feature a prominent minor third, the haunting *Miss You Much*, from the album *Rhythm Nation 1814* (1989), is practically an ode to that interval. If the opening is "shot like an arrow through my heart," then the rest of the track is about irritating that sore spot: pinning the arrow in place, plunging it deeper. As she launches into a series of minor thirds, Jackson even sings "I just know that it feels wrong," marking the song's move into imperfect consonance. That wrong feeling will be stressed again and again as the vocal keeps oscillating between first and third tones, nagging at the gap without resolution. The minor third cuts slanting lines through the track, giving menace to Jackson's declarations of love — her promises sound more like threats. *Miss You Much* is sung by a persistent lover who holds nothing back, telling "anyone whose heart can comprehend" about her longing, and how good it is to come home to a warm male carer (she chugs the word "go-go-go-go-good" like rich cocoa). If phone calls aren't enough, she will haul in his friends and even his mother to testify to their love — towards the end, we can't help but recall the mother when she cries "ma, ma, ma" over the bridge. There appears to be no such thing as emasculation here: only the drama of going big and public with desire.

Musically, the song is about an unbalanced intensity of focus: repeating the one phrase, slicing at the same target until a groove is formed. Unstable chords indicate the restlessness of a woman who won't stop until the whole world knows how she feels. While her voice sometimes trembles to show recoil from an arrow, the overriding impression is of sternness ("M-I-S-S you much"): spelling out words, schooling you, training your lips and body before the brain has time to resist. As in *What Have You Done for Me Lately,* there is also a beautiful "break" session — a time out that signals a sensual detour from the masterclass, through a segue into a major key. But this is only a calculated moment of tenderness before the militaristic beats re-array themselves.

During the promotion for this record, Janet was surrounded by muscular male dancers while maintaining a very covered image — an unrevealing black suit and cap, a closed body with a ripe, effulgent face. Believe it or not, this felt erotic at the time: a woman concealed and shaded, but with burning, outsize passions. She is physically unknowable, yet insists on shouting love from the rooftops, to the point of dragging the guy's mother into the equation. At one point, she breaks away from the tune to sing melismatically over the beat — a long wail that retraces all the notes sung hitherto.

Today, a female pop star who wore this much and sang this stridently might be seen to have "issues." A woman who doesn't make the basic effort to titillate is often seen as making a political statement — generally a humorless and tiresome one. If she won't even gyrate, she can hardly be regarded as a serious player in the industry. But at the time of *Rhythm Nation*, both Jackson's music and choreography reflected a guarded sexiness: cagey about what to reveal and when. Even the most sensual track on the album, the ballad *Someday is Tonight*, deals in a mix of emotions that would be unusual these days: its vibe is both horny and virginal, anything but zipless.

In her subsequent albums, from *The Velvet Rope* (1997) to *All For You* (2001), *Damita Jo* (2004), *20 Y.O.* (2006), and *Discipline* (2008), Janet's persona would become much more resolved: knowing, sultry, and less intriguingly divided. The songs turn increasingly to erotic play — and the response from critics and audiences has been mixed. Part of this may be the discomfort with desire in a mature woman, although her much-replayed "wardrobe malfunction" has not helped. In baring a breast at the 2004 Super Bowl, Jackson made three grave errors: exposing flesh deemed to be imperfect, being candid when she should have played coy, and worst of all, showing an insensitivity to market conditions. Immediately, her sexuality became a punchline.

Jackson's later songs do have a blend of eros and earnestness: a combination that is easy to mock. The highlight of *Damita Jo* is the underrated *Strawberry Bounce*, a track so flagrant it risks being risible. The song's title is in the tradition of Prince's *Raspberry Beret*, *Scarlet Pussy*, and *Pink Cashmere*: all hot colors and lush pillow. The "la-la-la-la" of the chorus is patently an inducement to cunnilingus, with its suggestion of a light, lapping tongue. Words are as prized for the delicious shapes we can make with our mouths as their content. As in *If*, not all the lyrics are intelligible, and those that are tend to be vivid nouns: "lips," "taste," "honey." Janet's deep, slurred voice contrasts with the tinkling notes of the glockenspiel — a deft little phrase that hops around mischievously while backing vocals repeat the line "lose control." Overall there is the impression of too much stimuli — too many high and low phrases being played at different speeds; a seductive sense of confusion. *Strawberry Bounce* may be one of Janet's more notorious romps, but the fact that it expresses lasciviousness through rhythm and texture as well as lyrics makes it memorable.

In recent years, Jackson has enjoyed a critical resurgence, with reviews praising her return to Jam and Lewis for *Unbreakable* (2015) after a stint with producer Jermaine Dupri. In truth, nothing on this album reaches the heights of *Control*, *Rhythm Nation*, *janet* (1993), or *The Velvet Rope*. The last time a Jackson single felt truly strange — and therefore approached greatness — was *Together Again* (1997). Janet's best songs are puzzling — torn between conflicting values, didactic yet ambiguous. They work with music's "speaking" qualities: the way a song can signal, even without words, that it is getting fed up and going through the motions, that a phrase is being drawn out against its will. In *If*, the would-be adulteress stays prim during the chorus ("I can't and I won't") while smuggling her real message underground, through muttered sweet nothings and obscenities we can barely make out. The Brothers in Rhythm mix also plays with music's ability to displace frustration, using beats to mark token time until lift-off. *What Have You Done for Me Lately* and *Nasty* demonstrate power via the jab of a chord — the latter makes a musical case for applying a nasty groove to nasty boys, cuffing them with the beat. *Miss You Much* alternates between storming power and delicacy: counter-intuitively, the singer's statement of love is an assault on the ears.

Dance explains some of the underlying oppositions in Jackson's music. Her signature freeze and drop — striking a harsh pose before momentarily relenting — is like a gun that stays pointed until everyone is disarmed. During *Control* and *Rhythm Nation 1814*, Jackson's performance style was based on stealth: the electrified, hyper-alert moves, the cross-body swipe suggesting a soldier's strap. Visually and rhythmically, dance was about training the body in ways that the brain might not comprehend. The choreography was full of strange, flag-like hand signs: holding up a certain number of fingers, closing and opening the palms to show "on guard" or "at ease." The title *Rhythm Nation 1814* was itself a disguised signal (R and N being the 18th and 14th letters of the alphabet, 1814 the year *The Star-Spangled Banner* was written), but even if you didn't know the code, the music promoted a particular kind of defense. The first, slashing notes of *Miss You Much* and *The Knowledge* arched your back and had you stalking like a cat, waiting to consolidate each move. Before you knew it, your body was schooled in the correct energies, able to control and release on demand.

Post-1990s, Jackson's music doesn't have the same fascinating tension between rigor and relaxation. That dynamic last made itself felt on *Together Again*, the second single from *The Velvet Rope*. The track was an enormous hit, yet it remains somewhat bizarre — according to Jackson it is an optimistic song, predicting a release from pain for AIDS sufferers. The video begins with the singer alone in a desert, then quickly switches to a utopian grassland, where giraffes and elephants graze alongside Janet's diverse group of friends. The lyrics are generic on paper ("Dancin' in moonlight, I know you are free / 'Cause I can see your star shinin' down on me"), but in combination with a hustling house beat, they are supremely addictive.

Together Again is uncanny in the way it balances two sets of interests. On the one hand, it wants to express patience and empathy, while on the other, it wants to get moving at all costs. The former is achieved through a beatific melody and a mood of expansive timelessness ("There are times when I look above and beyond / There are times when I feel your love around me, baby.") Jackson's grief for victims of AIDs is evident, yet these loving wishes are hurried away by the beat — the last line of the chorus is cut off on an ascending note, as the song rushes to stay on schedule. It is a contradiction that the ear is repeatedly drawn to: the languor of the melody on top and the relentless beats that drive it away. The song is torn between its sincerity and its impatience: the need to get to the next phase, when another layer of drum programming slides in. The lyrics — sometimes touching, sometimes perfunctory — might verge on insipid if it weren't for all this multi-tasking. The spaciousness suggested by the chorus ("Everywhere I go, every smile I see") is undercut by so much breathless pedaling underneath; the song might allude to a journey, but it is very brisk about collecting sights and sounds.

The video intensifies this duality: a hectic dance routine alternates with shots of Jackson majestically reclining, Cleopatra-style, on the African plain. Beats pound against the leisurely scenes. A Janet with two faces appears — one smiling, one sleeping. It's an image that reflects the song's central enigma: the prospect of heartfelt words being uttered automatically. In fact, the opposing concerns in this track ensure that good will never cloys — the chorus always seems to pull out too soon.

As with the great *If*, *Together Again* reveals itself to be a monumental work of restraint in the end. The song conjures a laidback fantasy that nevertheless obeys a strict meter. The power of that meter becomes evident when the chorus is cut short one last time. Instantly, energy levels drop to zero — a thunderclap has us stranded back in the desert. This is our final vision: that a dream of diversity and tolerance can be jerked away without warning, as if it never happened. Like *If*, the song is unflinching about closing on a note of shocked withdrawal. That's discipline.

KATE BUSH: THE RUPTURE

Today, Kate Bush is a genius no-one contests, but what was the oddness of the woman's first appearance on TV, and the even greater strangeness of her success as a pop star? When, in the *Wuthering Heights* video, that figure first appeared — a slash of red in the forest, a warning flash in its eyes — it was the visual equivalent of a shriek over jarring chords. The smashing effect of that encounter — still alarming, not yet normalized — has yet to be matched in popular music. Part of the mystery was the way that the initial shock eased into an insistently catchy refrain ("It's *me*, I'm Ca-*thy*"). The segue to a hip-swinging, if unconventional, chorus was a sign of this apparition making itself at home, treating all of its newness — its musical innovation, stark look and specific references – as a given.

For a musician known for her layered work in the studio, Kate Bush is surprisingly hummable — almost addictively so. None of the other women in this book is in any danger of winning a Nobel Prize, though Bush might, and her list of high-flown muses — Joyce, Brontë, Delius — would only seal the deal. But what made this peculiar artist "universal" has more to do with her pop instincts than her sophistication. So many of her iconic tracks, from *Running Up That Hill* (1985) and *Rubberband Girl* (1993) to *Babooshka* (1980) and *The Wedding List* (1978), are a mix of the handmade and the machine-tooled: beneath the fine lacework of these songs is a driving rock motor, the aggressive kick of popular music. It is the pairing of flash with delicacy that makes the work uncanny: the fact that these fey stories are infused with the rush of power pop. Her sensibility is inseparable from big drums, gaudy effects, and all that synth.

Bush may regret the arrangement of some of the Eighties and Nineties tracks — on the revisionist album *Director's Cut* (2011), she strips eleven previous songs of their period stylings, going for a "warmer, fuller" tone with analogue equipment — but while the engorged sound of Eighties superproduction may be too much for modern tastes, it is also a part of the songs' immediate appeal — in a word, their "wow." The 2011 version of *Rubberband Girl* suffers most from this deflation: the original single was arresting precisely because its deluxe sound matched the lyrical theme of impersonality. Instead of a refined treatment, the protagonist's fragility was wedded to glam excess. *Rubberband Girl* doesn't need warming up, any more than one would wish to "cleanse" Prince's work of its Eighties dazzle. Where would those songs be without their excitement over outdated technical wizardry, their exhausted spells?

Running Up That Hill is remarkable for the way its epic theme of alienation is expressed through modish pop effects, courtesy of the Fairlight synth. Rather than sounding dated, the song seems mysteriously timebound, as if an "eternal" subject was making itself known through the styles and forms of one period — in this case, Eighties melodrama, with its storm of agonized synth.

Bush's most enigmatic tracks are actually some of her catchiest. We marvel at the fact that such originality can be combined with the sure delivery of pop satisfaction: the chord progressions that give us catharsis, sometimes with the confected sadness of Japanese TV themes. Her lyrics read respectably off the page, but they are animated by startlingly aggressive hooks. *Babooshka* is extraordinarily cool about narrating a wife's devilish plan, using a little slip of a rhyme ("a pseudonym / to fool him") for exposition, and then plunging into the irresistible, sing-along chorus that fires the woman's rage. *The Wedding List* makes its tale of revenge murder almost comically accessible, especially during the coda: "And after she shot the guy / She committed suicide / And later when they analyzed / They found a little one inside." This sunny, swinging outro has us fairly dancing out the door. How natural and easy it is to pass over mere facts, carried along by the smooth line and the logic of rhyme.

The songs are particularly interesting in these "rocking" moments: listen to the use of power chords and boogie in *James and the Cold Gun* (1978), or the sax break in *The Saxophone Song* (1978) that wouldn't be out of place in Sade. Bush's lyrics can be so elegiac that they need the jolt of a riff. The result is a fully enclosed vision that also has the melodic drive and organization of a hit.

It is the tension between conventionality and strangeness that makes the work so absorbing. Bush's greatest songs tend to be based on a desperately simple wish: to be in love and never out of it, to be made instantly wise without effort (*Sat in Your Lap*, 1981), to have a test of love end happily (*Babooshka*), and the dream of sweet anesthesia in *Rubberband Girl* and *Running Up That Hill*. What these tracks have in common is the desire to rid oneself of complexity, to be relieved of one's history and memory. The narrator of *Running Up That Hill* claims that a body swap would lead to "no problems," and an ideal across several tracks is the serviceable "rubberband girl," capable of endless give. The goal is to be under a happy delusion: to think less and retain nothing, from a woman who unfortunately knows all too much. But the fantasy of ignorant bliss — à la *Westworld*, *Dollhouse*, or even *The Handmaid's Tale* — is seductive, and there are many ways of being a vacuum.

The woman in *Rubberband Girl* wants to switch from a feeling body to a cold machine, erased of all traces and trauma. She craves obliteration, longing to be never, forever. It is one of Bush's best and most suggestive lyrics, conveying the frantic, if insincere, yearning to be a pliant piece of ass (like the determinedly "empty" girl dreamed of by Stephen Malkmus in *Gold Soundz*, 1994). If the idea is to blank out the mind and let one's body take the hits, then the mode of contemporary dance seen in the video is the perfect solution. In the clip, Bush performs leaps and swoops under the care of a male dancer, who lifts her towards the temporary high of losing control. Dance gives one the chance to be completely elastic and yielding, then snap back in an instant. Why resist the system that moves you so efficiently? But too much rubber-banding can lead to a total loss of limits: by the end, the man sways Bush into a straitjacket, while the blare of the synth gives the sense of being pulled to breaking point. As in Bush's inspiration story, Hans Christian Andersen's *The Red Shoes*, each treacherous dance step corrodes the body.

The video for *Running Up That Hill* also looks at the ability to lose control as part of a choreography. In the arms of her male partner, Bush stretches and rises, making an "unfettered" leap under guidance — as close to elation as the song will get. In this track, a man and woman have reached that extreme point in their relationship where "a deal with God" seems like both the simplest and most audacious solution. Bush's character proposes a swapping of souls, so that her partner might know how she experiences pain. This plan, immature yet intensely desired, is made convincing melodically. The chorus seesaws, rapidly alternating between high and low notes (especially on "swap our places"), giving the impression of switching between two poles, two sites of perception: an implied duophony. Released from her own personality, Bush pictures herself flying free, up to a point — little rushes of notes ("Be running up that road, be running up that hill, be running up that building") express that projected energy, as she suddenly longs to scale impossible heights. However, when we actually hit the notes "road" and "hill," their slight depression sends us on a frustrated dash towards the next object. Bush's character imagines that life in a boy's body would be magically uncomplicated: full of eager, openhearted bounding, a child-like state of having "no problems." The grown woman knows things can't be that simple, but she retains the image of that free run, even if the song never gets her all the way there.

Like *Rubberband Girl* and *Babooshka*, *Running Up That Hill* envisions no compromise between pain and its absence. At the outset, the narrator claims to feel nothing, although her statement sounds truncated, as in "...it doesn't hurt me." The following question, "Do you want to know how it feels?," hints at both sympathy and sadism. Imagining her partner's life to be painless, she wants him to have a taste of hurt, but for the purpose of getting them to a new level of understanding. The repeated run-ups of the chorus seem like attempts to test this program out. They are exercises in momentum, to the extent that Bush's rhythms are often underscored by dance movement.

In the medium of dance, all of the dreams in *Running Up That Hill* can be realized: body-swapping, infinite wingspan, the mirroring of each other's gestures, an abrupt loss of power followed by gains. A girl can turn to gaffa or rubber in a man's arms, only to regain her independence a second later. What dance also supplies is the sudden injection of energy: the kick inside the music, which is the urgency of commercial pop. This kind of lift-off — achieved melodically, or with a dance partner — is the soaring feeling of "no problems," a vantage point that the woman compares with her own bruised life. The chorus of oscillating highs and lows suggests that there is no middle way by which these perspectives can be reconciled. The song's vibe remains a fog of synth and abstracted human voices ("yeah, yeah, yo"), pierced by drums and the melodic line: the occasional flash of lucidity.

A concentrated spiral of a song, *Babooshka* doesn't generalize about the nature of male and female desire — instead, it offers a single, unrepeatable case history, in which a character designs her own downfall. A Russian woman writes heated love letters to her husband under an assumed name, both hoping and fearing they'll catch fire. The plan works only too well: the man is hooked, reading the letters with a "strange delight," as Bush pronounces with cat-like pleasure. Arranging a meeting, the woman dresses up as her idea of an exotic temptress, but her unmasking will be the ruin of both husband and wife.

This tale of self-defeating ingenuity would be riveting purely in terms of plot — a *Vertigo*-like take on the way we script our own disasters with diabolical precision — but what made the song a huge hit is also what makes it mysterious: the cool roll-over of rhyme that naturalizes the woman's actions, and the infectious, shouting chorus with which the husband gladly tosses away his marriage: "All yours, babooshka, babooshka, babooshka, ya-ya!" Although she didn't know it at the time, Bush's lyrics combined two words for grandmother in Russian and Greek, *babushka* and *yaya*. This coincidence only adds to the imagery. Beneath the siren's guise is the rage of the aging woman, both thwarted and satisfied by her husband's taking the bait. That is the song's horror: of a granny made sexless by her own literary invention, tearing off the veil of youth and beauty.

In the video, Bush wears a mythical "Russian" costume, a mish-mash of stripes, gold bikini, and headdress that passes for ethnic. Like the use of the word *babushka*, this is a misguided appropriation that works. Despite her elegant reputation, Bush is as much of a cultural magpie as Nicki Minaj (and she can be as wild in her fantasy Englishness as Minaj, hovering between Cockney, Celtic, and archly upper-class accents). Throughout her career, Bush has seized on exciting fragments out of context: she famously wrote *Wuthering Heights* (1978) after seeing the tail-end of a TV miniseries rather than finishing the book, and became attracted to the idea of Delius after watching the Ken Russell biopic. In this case, she chose *babushka* irrespective of its meaning, hearing a latent whoosh and fire — and even her own name — in the word, and extrapolated her version of a narrative from there. She "does" Russian in the way that Minaj might pull a Roman Zolanski, authenticity and chronology paling beside the sweeping effect of the vision. In *Babooshka*, Bush keeps the exposition light and cool with a series of neat rhymes, reserving all her power for the whirlpool of the chorus.

The economy with which Bush narrates bizarre events — the triple killing in *The Wedding List*, the tiny rhyme containing the seeds of tragedy in *Babooshka* — is part of their enduring fascination. On the title track of her 2011 album, she engages our emotions — if not our understanding — with the impossibly specific cry, "Let me hear your 50 words for snow!" Her best work will always be maddeningly particular and, just as importantly, catchy. Along with her prized visual imagination, she has the underrated ability to give feeling and comfort on demand: to pace us through a wildly original song with a series of rest stops (*Wuthering Heights*); to soothe and unnerve with the yearning line of a chorus (*Mother Stands for Comfort*, 1985); to defy melodic expectations and keep that disappointment ringing in our ears (*Running Up That Hill*). That knack of catching and releasing our instincts is what enabled Bush's songs to travel, no matter how obscure their subject. As with Bowie and Morrissey, her way with hooks is a weirdly essential part of her work, tying mystery to the compulsiveness of dance. Kate Bush's songs may be ethereal, haunting, and all those other adjectives applied to female artists, but above all, they are immediate. Their urgency takes strangeness for granted.

MY PRETTY POISON:
SHAKESPEARS SISTER'S *SACRED HEART* AND *HORMONALLY YOURS*

In 1989 a peculiar debut album was released, its songs explicitly crafted around the matching of two female voices, high and low. The soprano, Marcella Detroit, sang in an extravagant falsetto designed to contrast with the dead-flat intonation of Siobhan Fahey. Lyrically, one might guess that Detroit would play angel to Fahey's devil, and this is sometimes the case: with her harsh ungiving voice, Fahey can sound like a sadist, torturing Detroit into exquisite fluttery cries. Even their most commercial single, the uncharacteristically peppy *You're History*, starts and ends with Detroit stretching her voice in a series of agonizing contortions, while Fahey stays cool and suave within her low range. On the song *Twist the Knife*, Detroit's vocal exists largely to let us know that "it hurts"; throughout the album she releases wails and "ows," both pained and ecstatic.

Part of the pleasure of Shakespears Sister is listening to the shifting interaction between these two: playing Jekyll and Hyde, good cop versus bad, or coming together to defeat a common enemy. The album *Sacred Heart* sees the women taking on a parade of distinct characters. Depending on the context, they might evoke a princess and her captor (even if Detroit's voice is way too high and histrionic for a romantic lead), a pair of gorgon sisters, or the Fates (we get the feeling that Detroit could be appeased, but Fahey remains pitiless). Most strikingly, all the voices on this album have a powerful sexuality that is specifically linked to aging. Witch, maternal lover, vamp on her deathbed: these are roles that combine allure with decay and disgust. In today's pop landscape, age is a much bigger taboo than sex — therefore an album that thoroughly combines the two subjects is wondrous to hear.

The consensus on Shakespears Sister's origins is that former Bananarama singer Fahey — then known as a ditzy golden blonde — lowered her voice, plastered her face white, and wrote scathing lyrics, finding acclaim in the process. But despite these contrivances, this is a band of genuine idiosyncrasy, prepared to discomfit us on the deepest levels. Fahey's persona goes beyond goth into grotesque: even when her voice is dried and cracked, it continues to insinuate sex. In videos and performances, she is both lecherous and dead-eyed. It's a combination that traditionally inspires repulsion — and hasn't been seen again until the remarkable Azealia Banks — but in Shakespears Sister, sex tends to be accompanied by an image of horror.

The opening track, *Heroine*, is the key to establishing this blend of lust and impersonality. Fahey's protagonist fantasizes about rescuing her man from death, and invents various scenarios where this might happen: a freezing winter at midnight, a last-minute phone call and knock at the door. But something is off: why the insistence on these exact conditions, which are repeated over and over? Why does she keep saying "Oh, baby" in that tone, which sounds excited rather than fearful? Fahey offers her lover protection and sacrifice, but only on very specific terms. Between the "dead of night" and the "blue, blue flowers," everything must be visually right, and one wonders if the singer has betrayed her man in order to have the satisfaction of saving him. Women may dream of rescuing and being rescued, but this damsel has darker intentions than the male: she is closer to a Nick Cave-style murderer than a romantic maiden.

Fahey's vocal here is like a drill to the head. While her character appears to offer nurturing warmth and comfort, her delivery is flat as a tack: each syllable is studded in tight, as if through gritted teeth. When vows of love are recited in a cold, robotic voice, the situation seems not only unreal but forced. Fahey huffs like a sergeant, and the song is punctuated with other sharp sounds: a metronomic beat and a vibrato note from Detroit, which, when sampled, suggests emotion on tap. This is a ghastly version of romance, in which every gesture is pre-programmed and the scenery comes as part of the package.

In general, Detroit's vocals, with their over-the-top flounces, show up the disdain of the Fahey voice, which has no juice or looseness at all. A song called *You Made Me Come to This* implies a sexual tribute, but Fahey turns the title phrase into a curse. In *Heaven Is in Your Arms*, the refrain of "I will never leave you / I will never let you go" sounds more like a threat than an oath, dripping both honey and irony. When desire is expressed, it tends to be of the Joan Crawford kind, the love of a creepy mother figure.

One of the most arresting tracks on the album, *Electric Moon*, is equal parts passion and detachment. It presents neon imagery against a black landscape, which tends to be the color scheme for Shakespears Sister, as in *Heroine*, *Red Rocket*, and *Dirty Mind*. As the song starts, a male grunt ("huh") sets the rhythm, and Fahey begins an unusually delicate vocal, playing a tenderhearted lover who gets sentimental at night. But in this quiet atmosphere, it is the ready-made sounds that stand out: the "huh" noise, the bright click-clack beats, and Detroit's trill, which sounds like a synthesizer effect. Although the grunt communicates a specific feel — an urgency that has been dulled — it seems as if all the emotions here have been sampled and automated, including Detroit's aroused quiver, which provides pain on demand. Even Fahey's nostalgia ("I wanna

see the stars shine ... that old moon's got me in its spell")
is curiously rote and generic. Although this is ostensibly a
spiritual number, our overwhelming impression is of stark,
synthetic sounds against blankness. The last noises we hear
are the masculine "huh" and the click-clack, which conduct
their own mechanical romance as the song fades out.

In an even more impersonal vein, *Red Rocket* anticipates
the sci-fi tone of the band's second album, *Hormonally
Yours* (1992). This time Fahey takes on the role of grunting
timekeeper, but she doesn't sound too thrilled about
going to the moon; her "wow" (no exclamation mark) is
precision-honed and joyless. This isn't the zany posturing
of Janelle Monáe, for whom space travel acts as more of
a style and fashion element. For Fahey, sci-fi is never an
escape from overwhelming ennui. Although there is no
shortage of musical inventiveness on the album, this and
several other tracks end by repeating chorus to fade, which
only enhances the feeling of soulless iteration.

Perhaps the most difficult track to listen to is *Primitive
Love*, a cavewoman rant about not caring. This song, in which
a woman knowingly picks up a bonehead, is excruciating
— for good reason. We open with a thick ugly bass — the
most flatulent bassline ever recorded — and then harsh
beats that evoke a cheap setting, possibly a hen night at
a strip club. There are wolf-calls and whistles, noises that
are comically tiny against the bleat of the bass. Clearly this
song, on which Fahey has sole writer's credit, is designed
to repel on a gut level. What turns out to be monstrous,
though, is the main character, who has big blunt desires
and an outsize lust. The loud, tramping beats suggest bones
rattling and gorillas dancing; a woman who is truly panting
and primitive in her search for a lunk to "get me out of this
trance." There is no verse to explain the back-story for this,
as Fahey just keeps repeating her mission statement ("Ah
ha ha, I need a primitive love, yeah / A stone age romance").

Female artists rarely release songs this squalid, yet this track plays with our ideas of what constitutes sleaze and filth. Do we recoil from the directness of its message, as much as we do from the ear-splitting sounds of the bass?

Elsewhere, Fahey challenges our notions of love by drawing on a trope of old Hollywood. One of her persistent themes is the idea of a woman with a long romantic history redeemed by contact with a young lover, who offers fresh hopes and idealism. It is the paradigm of "man with a future, woman with a past" that we sometimes encounter in 1930s cinema but very rarely in music these days. This is the kind of fable where a witch grows young in the arms of a knight, or an aging diva meets a pure romantic lead — she is more Garbo than Gloria Swanson, since her situation is tragic and affecting. In *Heaven Is in Your Arms*, this character walks through the gallery of her past and re-encounters one of her favorite conquests: the one that got away, who haunts her with his sweetness. On *Sacred Heart*, the praise for the lover is even more over-the-top, so that the listener is placed in the position of this idealized but impersonal beloved. Fahey refers to herself as a "fallen angel," a brittle woman with a soft spot for just one guy. As in Mae West's films, men are the figures of sensitivity here: they provide youth, integrity, physical strength, ardor, and innocence.

The narratives of these two songs merge with a third: the single *Run Silent, Run Deep*, which is both epic and melodramatic. Fahey's voice is tough and leathery but suave, as she looks back on her life with the resigned air of a Marlene Dietrich. The descriptions of her love interest ("You're soft and naked / You're young and strong") imply that she is none of these things: she is cynical, worldly, and — given the goth and military references — probably clad in black leather, as Dietrich was for her execution scene in *Dishonored* (1931). The man she describes is a lover/

assassin whose vigor is both a threat and a turn-on, and fear and desire become increasingly confused. We never know whether she is aroused by her own killer or the prospect of death in general.

In *Heaven Is in Your Arms*, this mood of disorientation is created by the blurred bell sounds, echo effects and the long trailing guitar lines that suggest a hark back to earlier days. When Fahey's character becomes confused about who she is talking to ("Or was I just imagining things? It seemed so real / Something that you left behind"), she might be remembering any of the male figures in *Run Silent, Run Deep*, *Sacred Heart*, or even *Heroine*. They all coalesce into the same type, visually and emotionally. The entire album is a closed world, caught in a spiral of recurring thoughts and imagery.

In the Seventies and Eighties, pop songs were often sung from the point of view of an experienced courtesan, a Camille-like figure epitomized by Stevie Nicks, Johnette Napolitano, Randy Crawford, and often Debbie Harry. This was also the era of the "empathetic" prostitution song, in which Crawford or Tina Turner might invite us to share the struggles of a private dancer. The protagonists of these songs were both ravaged and romantic: wised-up, sated with sex, and with the kind of jaded glamour a teenager might envy. Now the wizened voice of experience has vanished from the music scene, at least as far as female stars are concerned. Today's pop singers may be "fierce," but any hint of age or weariness is eliminated from the image.

On *Sacred Heart,* Shakespears Sister go even further than the singers of past decades. Fahey creates a more convincing picture of glamour gone to seed than, say, Courtney Love, and fills it out with a startling level of narrative detail. Fahey plays the part of the ruined ex-beauty queen, but takes it into the bizarre and unpalatable. In *Run Silent, Run Deep*, she depicts herself as death warmed up by a young lover;

Primitive Love is sung by a grown woman who is all but foaming at the mouth, with a candid sexual greed not seen since Barbara Stanwyck in her 1930s Warners films. Given the current obsession with defining "classy" standards of female behavior, this model of crude, unevolved sexuality remains inspiring.

With their debut record, Shakespears Sister made the case for women with dirty and obvious minds. However, their following album, *Hormonally Yours*, takes up the poison pen in different surroundings. While most of *Sacred Heart* depicted a worldly woman trapped in dreams, *Hormonally Yours* seems to be set on another planet entirely. In this new universe — potentially an afterlife — dark thoughts and deviltry are the norm. From the start, one simply accepts that the future is now a black space and that the human race has largely dwindled down to two personality types: the puerile, witchy woman and the hero of sensibility (either an over-refined male, or the shrieky voice of conscience represented by Detroit).

While Siobhan Fahey's character remains determined to play the villain — like the Azealia Banks of *1991* and Taylor Swift on her *Reputation* album — she does so with a vein of rich, experimental humor. She comes across as a Shylock without the self-pity, determined to parody the concept of evil and show up the hypocrisies of the virtuous. Occasionally, that makes her blundering and tactless, but overacting is a risk when playing the devil incarnate.

That mix of clumsy honesty and savvy villainy is seen in the album's best tracks: *My 16th Apology*, *Black Sky*, *Let Me Entertain You*, *Emotional Thing*, and the hit *I Don't Care* (make sure to listen to the album version, since the single remix criminally simplifies its structure). The baroque *My 16th Apology* is narrated cheerfully from beyond the grave: a toxic love letter written in lacy cursive script. Fahey gives her vocal a cloying sweetness, heavily enunciating each word while Detroit trills like Tweety Bird at the edges. Other than "I didn't mean to hurt you," which Detroit sings with happy abandon, every word is acid. The "apology," presumably sung to an unforgiving listener, is really more of a boast, in which Fahey invites admiration for the stylistics of evil — for the shimmering "streak of meanness" outlined in the chorus, the "river inside the size of my rage," and the marvel of possessing such qualities at a "tender age." The tone goes beyond irony into grimacing farce: the song plays like a jingle or a ditty, with sunny strings that sweep us away after the chorus, and the idyllic "la-la-las" that carry us towards the final epitaph: "Didn't your mother ever tell you / To err is human, to forgive is divine / Oh well, I'll see you in the next life."

I Don't Care begins with a long, high cry from Detroit: a wail that is like a preview of coming horrors. After three iterations of the jangly chorus, in which Fahey touts a light-hearted version of sadism ("We hurt the ones we love the most / It's a subtle form of discipline"), we hear that cry again and it triggers us back to the start, as if that opening was only a flash-forward in a sequence of nightmares. It's then that we have a strong sensation of being pulled downwards — underwater, as the bubbling sounds suggest, to a realm where Fahey, now using a noticeably different voice, holds court.

With a posh, plummy accent (as if she were nursing a cough drop in her throat), Fahey recites an extract from Edith Sitwell's poem *Hornpipe*, in which Queen Victoria disdains the glorious blackness of the goddess Venus: "This minx of course / Is as sharp as a lynx and blacker — deeper than the drinks and quite as / Hot as any Hottentot, without remorse! ... And the drinks, you can see / Are hot as any Hottentot, and not goods for me." Perhaps "minx" and "Hottentot" are insults in Victorian England, but coming out of Fahey's mouth they are delicious, caramelized treats.

Every "x" sound — in lynx, minx, drinks — is relished for its succulence. It's no surprise that Fahey is fascinated with rich shades of darkness, let alone that of the Venus who offends Victorian values — don't forget that in Bananarama, she sang of a *Venus* who was "black as the dark night" — but it is the way she communicates that delight vocally, as if savoring a long draught of black ink, that makes this interlude hypnotic.

While the single remix of *I Don't Care* is more of a straightforward rollicking number, ending on high spirits, the original album version closes with a reference to the afterlife. It is another warning epitaph, this time subtle and hard to make out. On closer listen, it has already begun during the final rendition of the chorus: "I know I'm going to see you there, in the land of..." is repeated, four times to fade. Earlier, the blithe message of the chorus ("I don't care if you talk about me / I don't care if you write it out in stone") has been undercut by Fahey's very insistent, precise diction. Here, as at the end of *My 16th Apology*, her character expresses a desire to see her nemesis in the next life — and who knows what destiny might have in store? So much for not caring...

The album, in its look, sound, and lyrics, is aesthetically aligned with blackness as beautiful and luxurious, like a sable coat. This culminates in the lush *Black Sky*, which fairly wallows in the conventional imagery of wickedness. The song indulges the fantasy of evil as a separable quality, envisioned as "green eyes" on black, like a cat or a snake — the bass and synth suggest roiling, writhing, slithering — but Fahey sings with an omniscience that sees through hypocrisy, knowing that in the end, there's "no rest for the good, no use in pretending that love is in your blood." Detroit also distances herself from any literal link to the occult by repeating "I ain't gonna sing that devil shit."

The final section of *Black Sky* is broken by a series of electrical pulses and snaps that jolt us into a different awareness. From here the song continues directly into *The Trouble With Andre*: a character study of malignity. Andre, it seems, is a man who does pretend that love is in his blood, and it is the duplicity that damns him. But what are the exact crimes and secrets he is hiding? Is he a war criminal, a rapist or pedophile? Fahey keeps hinting darkly at unspeakable acts ("But I know...") that have been suppressed, far beyond the cartoonish notions of evil in *Black Sky*. As both women conclude, the real "trouble with Andre is his disguise" — and Detroit hits anguished notes on "disguise." For Shakespears Sister, sanctimony is a greater sin than any willful act. Better to play the villain or vamp outright than to be this kind of pious monster.

Let Me Entertain You is set in a lurid pin-up world, perhaps a sci-fi version of the fleshpots seen in the previous album's *Dirty Mind* and *Primitive Love*. The gaudy synth instantly conjures sleaze and tat, and it is regularly punctuated by woofs (like a gruffer version of a wolf-whistle). The song is at once risible and compelling, although it takes some time to reach its climax. After a few phoned-in tales of the city, Fahey gives her client a soulful invitation: "Don't you want to put your trust in someone who's not ordinary?" Her character is decidedly not ordinary, and the guitar swirls deliriously as she sings. For a moment there is a possibility of connection in this world, the chance of finding a fellow freak, but a woof cuts off the melodic line at its peak. A few more woofs, and we're back to the repetition of "let me entertain you," the lure of a VIP lounge at a strip club.

An unlikely mega-hit, *Stay* is a crazed piece of work, even by Shakespears Sister standards. Clearly constructed to showcase Detroit's soprano and Fahey's guttural alto, it takes the angel/devil binary to wild extremes. An ethereal opening chord works as an establishing shot, suggesting that we are on another planet (which the video confirms). Two voices battle for the soul of a sleeping male beauty: a nurturing if over-protective lover (Detroit) and the seductive demon (Fahey) who offers an atheistic reality check. Dressed in a silver-black catsuit, Fahey sells the attractions of nihilism and the dark side ("'Cause when you sleep at night / They don't hear your cries / In your own world"). Glitching in and out of focus, she approaches the sleeping man, at which point Detroit utters the great falsetto cry that is the song's catharsis.

Today, *Hormonally Yours* might be seen as camp or goth pop, but neither of those terms encompasses the real strangeness of the album, or the way it casually resets the poles of our universe. Somehow, this insanely detailed pantomime managed to capture the public's imagination. It now seems unbelievable that *Stay* spent two months at the top of the British charts, screening in video countdowns — the clip was even banned in Germany for showing witchcraft, being too frightening, and blasphemously raising the dead through black magic. Week after week viewers tuned in to this psychodrama, becoming torn — much like the comatose man in the video — between the suffering heroine and Fahey's dazzling fiend.

Throughout *Hormonally Yours* and *Sacred Heart*, Fahey and Detroit explore the moral and mythological implications of voice and sound. On *Stay*, Detroit's lofty soprano suggests a holier-than-thou persona, a martyr. It is an extension of the women's relationship in *Sacred Heart*, where Fahey tended to play the sadist with her obliging victim. For the rest of *Hormonally Yours*, the singers are more often in league: two witches cackling over their black brew. In *I Don't Care* and *My 16th Apology*, Detroit provides a cheer squad of the "You tell 'em, sister!" variety, musicalizing Fahey's spoken narrative. This ever-changing dynamic feeds the ambiguity of both albums.

Above all, there is the continuing uncertainty over Detroit's status in relation to Fahey. Is she an echo, an antagonist, or an alter ego? Do her shrieks tell Fahey she's gone too far, or are they a parody of girlish helplessness? The power game between the two keeps shifting, and tracking their relationship turns into a game of bait-and-switch. Through their multiple personae, Shakespears Sister launched a series of extreme archetypes — the cold-eyed woman looking for a pick-up; the crone grown perversely sexy in her dotage; the devoted heroine who might also be the villain. And they were able to parlay these roles into mainstream success in the Nineties, without being mocked! That in itself is worth marveling at.

NEW SHOES AND BLACK MOODS:
MICHELLE GUREVICH AKA CHINAWOMAN

The author of two superb, self-released singles in the 2000s, Michelle Gurevich has a white-telephone voice: the tone of a party girl in recovery, who can barely be roused to torture herself. It is as if Shakespears Sister's Siobhan Fahey had gone high society and full glamour, and become increasingly self-lacerating in the process.

Russian Ballerina (2007) and *Party Girl* (2007) are songs of compromised relationships, mostly with oneself. Both deal with a desire to be the kind of "rubberband girl" described by Kate Bush: the woman who can simply snap back from anger, passion, and artistic ambition to become a more malleable, pleasing version of herself. The narrator of *Party Girl* is an aspiring writer who has faced facts, realizing she needs to become the whole package. Now she is that rarefied creature, the literary socialite, who has upgraded her personality from "fragile" to "so wild."

These spare studies of pain are accompanied by daringly minimal videos, which feature a sequence of grainy images on repeat, suggesting home movies watched to the point of addiction. The clip for *Party Girl* shows a woman making multiple attempts to descend a staircase on the arm of an older man, while being greeted by a throng of photographers — for a good twelve seconds, her face is obscured by the flashbulbs. She wears a precise, unchanging smile and a shimmering dress. Knowing exactly how to inhabit the eyeline, she executes a series of red-carpet poses, back muscles tensed to catch the camera. The entire video consists of re-takes of these moments: the postures, the looks, and that smile.

Party Girl might come across as stylized malaise, in the tradition of Dorothy Parker, if not for the melancholy that seizes us from the first chord. Almost all of Gurevich's work is set in an imperiled minor key. The guitar alternates between two chords, continuously generating and allaying suspense. Meanwhile, Gurevich's voice holds center stage. Her DOA delivery is somewhere between dry wit and a narcotized blankness, occasionally rising to brighten a word such as "heart" or "wild." Her very deliberate vocal style, making best use of a small range, is about pulling on odd sounds to dramatically inflect them, while downplaying expected emphasis.

This assured woman tells us she has a secret vein of sadness — a claim supported by her haunting repetition of the minor sixth, which creates a mood of desolation. She is perpetually worn out from socializing, tired of the arduous but necessary "fun" that goes into self-presentation. One reviewer nominated Gurevich as the "most theatrical" performer at the 2019 Tbilisi Open Air festival, noting that she "became so overcome with ennui during *Vacation from Love* that she had to sit down with her face in her hands while she sang."

For artists from Lana Del Rey to Scarlett Johansson to Billie Eilish, an air of world-weariness adds decorative finish to a young voice, like a vintage garment or a streak of grey hair that shows up the freshness of unmarked skin. A token husk or rasp dispels suspicions of callowness, marking the singer as precociously hardened and experienced (even if an audibly aged female voice is rarely heard today). With the heavy "folds" of her voice, Gurevich is no less affected than Del Rey or Johansson, but her version of apathy has a specificity and a hint of shabbiness we seldom find in English-language pop.

The Russian-Canadian singer, whose biggest following is in Eastern Europe, has grown up with 1970s Soviet pop artists such as Edita Piekha and Alla Pugacheva, and her work has absorbed some of the characteristics of Russian music of that period, with its unusual intervals, ostinatos, and harmonic minors. Together with the repeated actions in her videos, her chords tend to suggest restriction and stymied movement, being caught in a step-and-repeat. When Gurevich plays the shady lady, the faded prima donna, the allusions to age are melodic as well as lyrical.

In interviews, Gurevich has said that she "may actually be writing the same song over and over, still trying to get it right. It's usually about the ending of things, or the difference between how it was and how it is, the inevitabilities of time ... so many moments disappearing without leaving any trace." The singer of *Russian Ballerina* is lost in the fascination "between how it was and how it is" and its video is similarly fixated on the lack of trace. In lieu of production values or a budget, it simply repeats a ten-second clip of a trim, mature woman dancing, executing a neat series of spins.

The narrator, with a mixture of awe and dismay, tells the tale of her mother, a Soviet dancer who casually gave up her "allegiance to a life of art" in favor of a normcore existence in the US, "driving a Corvette." In a hyper-specific, expository chorus that doesn't rhyme ("Oh, my mother, Russian ballerina! You were a swan but now you're swimming in the Caribbean"), Gurevich does a seesawing vocal, performing contortions to get all the words and details in. This strenuous effort, it is implied, is needed to depict a character of such complexity: a woman who can simply reshape her interests to match the spirit of the times.

The singer's mother is a different kind of "party girl" — although she doesn't much socialize, she has calmly taken to a lifestyle of Americana, ease, and vacations. She has segued from her history of perfectionism to a new life of luxury and contentment, all while maintaining the looks and grace of a society swan. Watching the undulating woman in the video, we are placed in the position of the daughter, marveling at the serenity of a mother who can relinquish passion on demand, and seemingly move on without regret. As the duck-and-dive chorus explains, everyone wonders how you can "live without the love of your life." While upset about her mother's wasted talent — in particular, the squandering of star power — the daughter is shocked, even envious, at the lack of inner conflict.

The song itself is full of conflict and contradiction. As in *Party Girl*, the ostensible message might be the joys of simplification, but the singer can't help regretting the transition from artistic complexity to a publicly legible persona. The mother gave up her craft and her discipline to slide into the mainstream of American life; the party girl would like to do something similar, but doesn't have the ballerina's lightness of touch. *Russian Ballerina* shows an ambiguous attitude to high culture, valorizing dance but pronouncing a fancy word like "pirouette" or "milieu" with a degree of detachment — the verbal equivalent of touching it with tweezers — and even flattening out "milieu" to rhyme with "bamboo."

At the end of the track, Gurevich sings a catchy series of "la-la-las," reminiscent of Russian pop, which musicalize the mother's story and turn it into a trope. She is coolly matter-of-fact about introducing Eastern European clichés to the Western pop song ("One day it's eggshells and bread"), often knowingly leaning into stereotypes.

Gurevich recorded *Party Girl* under the alias Chinawoman — a dubious name and a historical slur to be sure, but one suited to the kind of brittle exotic she keeps on playing. "Chinawoman" evokes a creature of pure fantasy: a character out of pre-Code cinema, the femme fatale of Josef von Sternberg's *Shanghai Express* (1932) embodied by Anna May Wong and aspired to by Gurevich.

Over the years, the artist's habit of "writing the same song over and over" has in fact grown old — none of her recent work measures up to the 2007 debut album, recorded in her bedroom. Later songs such as *To Be with Others* (2014) and *First Six Months of Love* (2016) are lugubrious, their cynicism forced and insistent rather than reflexive. The singer seems too conscious of playing the brainy dilettante — the wiseguy snarl and noir lyrics of *Woman's Touch* (2010) are overly contrived. But on her debut, Gurevich's obsessive themes and compulsion for minor chords coalesced on two magical tracks.

Russian Ballerina and *Party Girl* are still utterly absorbing: lively and stimulating despite their mood of enervation. The twisted romance of her early work has been energizing for movie directors: *Party Girl* inspired the 2014 French film of the same title, while another song from the first record, *Lovers are Strangers* (2007), was used as the theme for *Kolka Cool* (2011). In spite of this relative success, Gurevich remains unreviewed by most of the major English-language outlets — she really is the outlier her songs project her to be. I first heard *Party Girl* while watching the French channel Fashion TV, which broadcasts runway shows as well as slightly dingy footage of parties packed with hopeful ingénues. It was an uncanny match: the song of a seasoned denizen accompanying shots of blank-eyed models and girls drinking sponsored champagne. All waiting for that elusive touch of stardom.

INTERLUDE: LOVE IS THE DRUG

The Genius of Love

A question that can be asked of any great record is, "Why *that*?" The best pop songs are not "universal," but unaccountably specific in their detail: in their lyrical hang-ups that correspond to the hooks of the chorus. Of all the notes released, why do only *Strawberry Letter 23* and *Love Potion No. 9* hit the sweet spot? Of all girls and groupies, why *Billie Jean* and not others? Only a precise sequence of sounds unlocks the secret to a hit: the magical iteration of *Bonita Applebum* and *Mister Dobalina* — the two great Alakazams of pop — that casts an irreversible spell.

Pop alludes to its own alchemical nature when it deals in these kinds of formulas and flavors, with the implication that there is a single combination that can elicit joy. It is through this strange specificity that a song makes its mark as indispensable, rather than just another work to add to the canon: one more finely honed verse or tight rap.

In particular, there seems to be an occult intensity around colors, numbers, and names. The early albums of Prince and Kate Bush have this sense of idiosyncrasy, marrying "timeless" themes with strangely exclusive references. Prince has been able to weave an entire universe around various shades of pink, purple, and peach, the numbers 2 and 7, and his personal sexual iconography. Yet, given the narrowness of these preoccupations, the songs are towering and expansive: anything but limited. It seems absurd that iconic work could grow out of such particular fragments, but the key may lie in the concentration that binds them all together. A song may be rooted in a quaint fantasy, but if that fantasy is inhabited with total depth and conviction, we too can be convinced that the world revolves around the color purple and the number 7.

Part of the mystery is a singer's ability to invest a sound with what seems like uncanny, superstitious power, lingering longer than they should over a commonplace word. The Johnny Mathis cover of *Route 66* — another classic involving a talismanic number — is a cruisy, hummable version of the standard, but the truly memorable bit comes at the end of the chorus, when Mathis makes a meal out of the word "six," savoring the thickness of every "x" and "s" sound.

Mathis works the friction of these consonants so that there is an almost palpable sweatiness about the track, rather than the cool swank of Nat King Cole's original. Striking effects like these may constitute our primary memories of a song, but they are hard to predict or orchestrate in advance. It all depends on the right impulse seizing the mouth as it meets the right word — and then for that slight distortion to call up responses in the listener.

Sometimes this kind of eccentricity in phrasing can rub critics the wrong way — Carly Simon has been mocked by the likes of Robert Christgau for her "clumsy" songs and unscannable lines. But there is a reason why at least two of her tracks have remained haunting over the decades: they have the necessary strangeness that makes for great or memorable work. *You're So Vain* (1972) is considered one of the biggest enigmas in pop, and not just because of the speculation surrounding its subject. Simon's take-down of a former lover is far from conventional — in order to identify the man without naming him, the singer inserts all kinds of descriptive details, to the point where they screw with the song's timings. "Yacht" is rhymed with "apricot," and words like "strategically" are crammed into the verse, throwing us off the beat (Christgau refers to these as "numerous syntactical awkwardnesses.") At one point, she even holds up the chorus to jam in this lengthy accusation: "And when you're not, you're with some underworld spy / Or the wife of a close friend, wife of a close friend." Quite a mouthful: not at all catchy, but totally in character, as if the narrator is determined to air all of her resentment at the expense of the song's momentum, squeezing in every word that comes to mind.

In her other great hymn to narcissism, *Nobody Does It Better* (1977), Simon again sings unconventional rhymes (this time written by Carole Bayer Sager), but in this case the song's meaning is adjusted to fit the meter. The phrase "Like heaven above me" is sung with apparent sincerity, but in the next line we see it is only a rhyme for the film it advertises, *The Spy Who Loved Me*. A throwaway couplet is inserted to keep timings neat, as well as to service the song's function as a James Bond theme.

These two songs don't fit any traditional model of good writing — especially if one believes in an orderly relationship between meaning and syntax — but they do open up new formal possibilities in their expressively slapdash use of language. *Nobody Does It Better* changes its content solely to accommodate a rhyme, while *You're So Vain* stuffs in as much as possible, elegance be damned. Both are just peculiar enough, with the sense of something accidental swept into the mix. That's why they've endured.

When it comes to making strangeness universal, Michael Jackson's *Billie Jean* (1982) is the prime example of a track rooted in a small, topical subject that has nevertheless shaped the collective imagination. How does a song about refuting a paternity claim turn into an epic assertion of identity, one of the greatest of all time?

First of all, the singer explains his entrapment by Billie Jean, his low, controlled voice indicating his desire to keep the matter private. According to the lyrics, he's embarrassed by the girl's allegations, but then the melody suddenly shoots up as he sings "I am the one," producing a contrary meaning: a strange momentary elation. The fact that the chorus hits its apex on "kid" and "I am the one" rather than during his denials ("not my lover," "not my son") shifts the song from its intention. Although the lyrics refute Billie Jean's claim, "I am the one" is where the melody crests, releasing the tension of the compressed verses, so that what should be a shameful admission is the song's crowning moment. Thus a straightforward defense is complicated, since the rhythmic emphasis is on what the singer *doesn't* want to hear (Jackson had to battle Quincy Jones' wish to rename the song *Not My Lover*, which would have removed some of the ambiguity). The narrator may be sure of his innocence, but his voice still packs the intensity of a primal struggle: the mixture of humiliation and pride over a beautiful woman.

Single Minds Can Think Alike

The classic minimalism of *Billie Jean* only draws attention to its oddities: its curiously specific central imagery, and the fact that a random pop culture reference (to a tennis player of the era, as in Saint Etienne's *Conchita Martinez*, 1993) is picked up and mythologized for no obvious reason. Jackson's attitude is one of defiance, yet the song rhythmically highlights the claims of his accuser. Unpacking the mysteries of this track involves trying to digest the emotional meaning of sounds — something that criticism has historically been reluctant to do. Today, the majority of album reviews don't spend more than a couple of adjectives defining tone and timbre. They nail down what's concrete: the instruments, the stated subject of the lyrics, a curated list of influences. They are happy to discuss verbal irony, but not, for instance, an ironic juxtaposition of sounds — a melody's ability to scramble and contest the speaker's message. Perhaps there is the conviction that all images associated with sound must be "subjective," and are therefore beyond the purview of the objective critic. There is also the realistic fear of being mocked for going too far with descriptions, in the manner of a wine writer or a psychic.

This line of thinking can be summarized by the notorious quote from musical comedian Martin Mull (echoed by Elvis Costello) that "talking about music is like dancing about architecture" — in other words, it's not only pretentious but fundamentally wrong-headed. Never mind that many of the great choreographers of the last century — Merce Cunningham, William Forsythe, Twyla Tharp, Mark Morris — do in fact construct dance about architecture. If mainstream journalism doesn't have a problem with wine being "chewy" or "leathery," and prose is routinely described as "chiseled" and "diamond-hard," then I fail to see why music descriptors come in for special scorn.

In any case, it seems absurd to suggest that music and voices don't come with any implied imagery. If we concede that words have aesthetic, sensual connotations apart from their grammatical function, then surely songs have the same capacity, with their added variables of pitch, rhythm, and timbre. Even the slightest identification with a singer's delivery would lead the listener to experience sensations in the mouth, a tang on the tongue. How could hearing a wall of fuzz not bring up visions of texture?

In film studies, it has become a cliché to favor the pop pleasures of Frank Tashlin and Douglas Sirk over the grand intentions of a John Ford. We now understand that comedy is at least as difficult to pull off as drama, and that great performances need not show strain or virtuosity. Yet in music, elegance and gravitas are values that still command automatic respect. Most of our lauded artists fit the mold of muse or raconteur — the critical preference is for music that tells you it's serious rather than a song that declares itself vapid and proceeds to undo that assumption.

Poetic pacing and cryptic word choices are the surest routes to applause, even when paired with your standard chord progressions. Genius is seen as masterly rather than silly, wiggly or funky — the wonderful exception is Prince, but until his death, his work rarely received sound-by-sound analysis. There is a bias toward the painstaking, carefully constructed sentence versus the unaccountable and irresistible riff, the one-two patterning of notes that repeats and repeats in your ear. A crazily infectious song that rhymes "tune" with "soon" or "miss you" with "kiss you" has little chance of being regarded seriously, unless it has the austere structure of *Billie Jean* or Chic's *Everybody Dance* (1978): two of the rare danceable tracks to make it onto canonical lists.

But verbal ingenuity is only one approach to songwriting — and shapely sentences need to be fused with addictive sounds. Words are important, but not only for their literal meaning: just as interesting are the fond lingering on syllables and the delectation of certain sounds. Take Michael Jackson's posthumous single *Love Never Felt So Good* (2014), sublime in both demo and remix. Pleasure begins at once, when Jackson sings the title phrase with his trademark gasping urgency. "Good" is pronounced strong and true, but on the second iteration, Jackson sings "love never felt so *fine*," putting a little nuanced texture on "fine," the equivalent of a backhand spin in tennis. Throughout the song his voice will continue to explore the idyllic nature of the word "fine," throwing a ripple of vibrato here and there. The ear delights in these endless subtle variations of timbre: smooth and matt, clear and shaded. Then, in an ascending bridge, Jackson lets us know that he's "gotta fly."

It might be considered trite to sing "fly" when your own voice is soaring, but in this case, who can resist such wings? (Even the famously fussy Radiohead weren't above this kind of uplift in *High and Dry*, 1995).

Next we come to the chorus, which is sung so imploringly that we may not notice (or care) that it doesn't make sense: "Tell me, if you really love me / It's in and out my life / In out, baby." Is it love that rushes in and out of life, or something else? Whatever "it" is, it has condensed down to "in out" by the end of the chorus. Thanks to Jackson's passionate delivery, the elliptical phrasing works: while its meaning is unclear, the line "In out, baby" evokes an intense plunge, a propulsion. Though we may not understand why, everything is on the line here: feelings are coursing in and out with the momentum of the song. Would the lyrics really work better if they were more coherent or cleanly articulated? Probably not, since we wouldn't get the same sense of euphoria sweeping away common sense — and if anything, this song is a master-class in lightness.

The Sensual World

Since music criticism has traditionally been suspicious of exuberance, the most underrated songs are necessarily those that lack a veneer of sophistication, making them harder to defend as art. Case in point: look at the contrast in reputations between David Byrne's Talking Heads and Tom Tom Club (featuring Byrne's former bandmates Tina Weymouth and Chris Frantz). With his biting sarcasm and wit, Byrne fits the mold of the heroic satirist: his talents are renowned and rarely disputed. However, Weymouth's place in history is much less secure. She is the major creative force behind Tom Tom Club's cult hits, *Genius of Love* (1981) and *Wordy Rappinghood* (1981), but both of these songs are far from polished: they take a soft approach to language.

Watching the Talking Heads concert film *Stop Making Sense* (1984), I was struck by the extreme contrast in styles when Byrne cedes the stage to Tom Tom Club for a number. Most of the film is driven by Byrne, who hurls out ironic slogans in a pumped-up series of songs: *Life During Wartime, Burning Down the House, Once in a Lifetime*. Byrne's delivery is undeniably powerful and his nonstop energy makes for an exhilarating film, but the air changes dramatically when he leaves and bassist/singer Weymouth comes forward with *Genius of Love*. This song is introduced as a "girls can do it" interlude, a palate cleanser (director Jonathan Demme included it mainly to facilitate Byrne's costume change). It adds an injection of mood and magic to an otherwise relentless show.

Byrne's authoritative speeches give way to a mysterious assembly of voices, as Weymouth and her backing singers sing to each other in light, chirrupy tones. Their cooing vocals sound deceptively tame and submissive — especially since the lyrics describe a female inmate who is about to be released from jail, anticipating "fun, nasty fun." It isn't clear whether the vocal line represents the thoughts of this one woman, a group of girls, or a state of mind not attached to a particular character. And does "nasty" just mean sexual, or does it refer to the cocaine madness that led them to jail in the first place? There is a suggestion of malevolence and danger behind the gentle intimacy of the vocals, even though what dominates is an image of serene tropical life, created by the piping synth and tom-toms. The singers come across as both "nasty" felons and lotus-eaters; they chirp at each other like harmless little birds, but that unreal highness seems to be the effect of denial, if not a drug bender.

The studio version of the track features Weymouth and her two sisters twittering over the island beat, at one point breaking into gibberish: apparently a mythical language one of the sisters invented as a child. As in Deee-Lite's *Good Beat* (1990), there is an excitement about smuggling a secret language into global pop: a jabber that is incomprehensible, but sounds internally consistent and lived-in. Most importantly, this nonsense tongue is rhythmically right: an utterly personal creation that is also a catchy hook.

With *Genius of Love*, *Stop Making Sense* takes a detour into sensuality that fades once Byrne returns to the stage. Byrne's precise articulation and deft lyrics suggested a very guarded, self-conscious intelligence, which is the opposite of Tom Tom Club's strange interplay of voices. Unlike most of Talking Heads' music, *Genius of Love* has never really been decoded and thus continues to fascinate. We can hear where Byrne is coming from — a place of sardonic anger — but who knows what frequency Weymouth is tuned into? Is it even human?

Genius of Love has been sampled by everyone from Grandmaster Flash to Public Enemy to Mariah Carey, yet it does not appear on "best" lists with the same frequency as *Once in a Lifetime* (1980), Byrne's very quotable ode to midlife crisis ("And you may tell yourself, this is not my beautiful house! / And you may tell yourself, this is not my beautiful wife!"). We rarely hear Weymouth or her collaborator Chris Frantz mentioned among the great songwriters — that accolade belongs to Byrne and his monologues. It might be said that Weymouth's "instinctive" style is just as much of a conceit as Byrne's cerebral one, but it's clear that Tom Tom Club and Talking Heads have very different lyrical approaches, as signaled by their respective bandnames.

Naturally, there is room for both Byrne's and Weymouth's takes on popular music — for Byrne's discrete characters and thoughts as well as Weymouth's blur of identities. Yet Tom Tom Club is generally seen as a side project or curious cousin of Talking Heads, despite the immense contribution of *Genius of Love* alone; Robert Christgau describes the band as a "career alternative that lets them feel useful when David goes off on a tangent." Weymouth's penchant for making airy, left-field remarks to journalists ("Do you like our dahlia? It's good!") has probably not helped, but too often the musical canon venerates the same old stinging monologues and obvious cynicism (*Once in a Lifetime*, Bob Dylan's *Like a Rolling Stone*, 1965, and Nirvana's *Smells Like Teen Spirit*, 1991, tend to vie for the top spot). Weymouth sees lyrics as a bunch of sound effects and image associations, rather than an orderly procession of meanings. Why is that approach so little valued?

Tom Tom Club's other signature hit, *Wordy Rappinghood*, claims to have a flip attitude to language, opening with a rhetorical question ("What are words worth?") that is nevertheless a play on a poet's name. In fact, this song does have literary antecedents, although its lyrical inspirations are more likely to be Gertrude Stein and Jane Bowles, in its use of a child-like inner voice to highlight the automatic quality of language ("words that write the book I like.") Words are out of control, forming sentences beyond the speaker's comprehension; language is a perpetual motion machine that eludes authorial purpose.

Singing leads Weymouth into unexpected territory; sampling an overheard phrase, she finds herself rapping in a tone of prim disapproval before switching back to her "artless" voice. Despite the occasional Byrne-like dig ("words have nearly always hung me," "words are like a certain person who can't say what they mean"), the song's hold on common sense and on the English language is precarious. Lapsing into French, Weymouth even insists that meanings can be juiced on demand ("*mots pressés, mot sensés*"). This is a unique lyrical style, rejecting the beauty of carved sentences in favor of rhythmically structured babble.

In a 2013 conversation with *Salon*, Byrne spoke in favor of singing "gibberish" and "emotional, verbal utterance" that eludes the "rational faculties"; his interviewer, David Daley, praised him for recognizing that "the way a word sounds and rings in a song carries its own emotional impact ... more feeling than what the word itself means." Byrne's own manifesto *How Music Works* also asserts that the meaning of songs is "sometimes in the words, but just as often the content comes from a combination of sounds, rhythms, and vocal textures that communicate ... in ways that bypass the reasoning centers of the brain and go straight to our emotions." Beautifully put, but if any 20th century song demonstrates this ethos, surely it is *Wordy Rappinghood*.

In her lyrics, Weymouth tends to present a childish, barely defended self, with a deceptively plain turn of phrase. For *Wordy Rappinghood*, she refers blithely to language as "words to tell you what to do" and marvels at the "words of nuance, words of skill" practiced by other people. Weymouth allows herself no critical distance from this character, for whom self-expression is always a puzzle. Language is limber, never stuck in rigid poses or structures, and this allows the song to pass through a range of dream-like moods: erotic, babyish, demurely polite (towards the end, she even solicitously says "Bye!" to listeners — can you imagine Byrne doing that?). Because of these high-spirited flourishes, Weymouth's work risks being seen as a fun novelty rather than the major achievement it is. But make no mistake, *Wordy Rappinghood* is the Open Sesame of pop: the chant that discloses a vast interior world inaccessible to logic.

The track begins with the noise of bashing typewriter keys and a voice asking, "What are words worth?" But this is no author suffering from style fatigue — instead, it's the introduction to a world of pop language, in which words jump around like excited particles to a dance beat. As a keyboard riff inches forward, sounds circulate, breaking up and re-forming in crazy combos. According to the lyrics, words are like coinage, constantly being exchanged, processed and divvied up for food. Weymouth's vocal explains that, under this system, "words are working hard for you," but her voice doesn't hold much authority: she has the staccato tone of a cross little child. When her sisters Lani and Laura start chiming in, they sound like a band of excited girls who have picked up a bunch of ideas and shaped them into a nursery tune.

Some sophisticated notions are presented, including the concept of automatic writing ("words that write the book I like"), but the girls retain a fearsome simplicity when it comes to the tactile enjoyment of language: they say a word because it feels good to say it. You can hear the smack of lips as they sing, "Panty, toilet, dirty devil"; for the Weymouths, words carry the same sexy and illicit charge they did in childhood.

After a verse in praise of language's multi-tasking abilities, the girls leap into the following chorus: "Houdi qouri houdi qouri ram sam / Haykayay yippie yaykayé / Ahoo ahoo a hikichi." This babble is not completely indecipherable: "ram sam" comes from the well-known children's game, and we can pick out the notes of triumph in "yippie yaykayé." Sung in catchy unison by the sisters, it is both confounding and strangely addictive: a nonsense chant made logical by its familiar rhythms, drawing us into the synchronized madness of a group of young girls.

As it happens, this chorus does have its origins in childhood. Growing up, the three Weymouth sisters were given to holding hands and singing songs while exploring their French town. During their walks, they often overheard a chant they couldn't understand. The three of them would incorporate fragments of the chant into their singsong, trying out different combinations until they reached a version they could agree on. Only later did they realize they were copying a North African song, making their own selections and approximations of the foreign words.

Years later, when recording their debut album, they were having trouble with the chorus of *Wordy Rappinghood*. One of the sisters began spontaneously humming the song from their childhood, which they had long forgotten about. The three women realized they could still sing this theme identically on command, and it became a naturalized part of the song, melding into the verses without a break.

We don't need to know this story to become enchanted by *Wordy Rappinghood*. Somehow, from the first round of "ahoo a hikichi," we know we're not hearing just any old blather, but a lyric with the force and compression of a spell. The chorus seems not only whimsical but eerie, with the quality of something intimately known and possessed. The mind can make no sense of the words, but they repeat effortlessly on the tongue, as if we'd always known them. Why is this?

When the Weymouth girls first heard the African chant, they began to mimic it unthinkingly, like lyrebirds: who knows whether they were imitating a prayer or a hello, one voice or twelve? They copied the words they could pronounce and garbled the ones they didn't, improvising again and again until they reached the version they found nicest to sing. Over time their chant became refined, resolving down to its core sounds, like a smooth stone worn into accessible grooves. The result is a series of incomprehensible words that are nevertheless easy for an English speaker to digest, since they have been scaled down to the structures of a nursery rhyme. The song that emerges is the one that has remained memorable through years of experimentation, burning through the field of other possible combinations. It contains the distillates of multiple tongues, and is sung with a deep sense of attachment. Whether or not we realize it, this is "nonsense" that is specifically patterned to appeal to our instincts.

Such secret recipes are hard to come by. At its best, pop relies on a sequence of sounds that is both gripping and unaccountable, but it is rare to come across a chorus that entirely defeats rational intelligence. You can imagine asking a writer to pen a Talking Heads-style polemic on the evils of consumerism, a smart anthem covering the issues of the day. It might not be as good as David Byrne, but it would be feasible. However, commissioning a song on the level of *Wordy Rappinghood* or *Genius of Love* would be close to impossible. One could presumably write a vaguely foreign-sounding chant with naïve lyrics, but would the mouth take to it so naturally, like a language one had forgotten? Even though authenticity is of questionable value in music, how would you replicate a lived-in theme that represents the aggregate of three memories?

The small and intimate magic of these two tracks is a precious, perhaps finite, resource. If Tom Tom Club never reached those heights again, that may be due to the mysterious felicity of pop, which boasts more one-hit wonders than any other art form. The world of music needs the flash in the pan as much as the focused artist, to show how disparate elements can come together and *hit*, defying the conventions of songwriting. As a result, the secret code of three sisters has become an underground cult, sung and transmitted by clubbers everywhere.

STARTS WITH TLC:
OBSCENITY AND NUANCE IN HIP-HOP

At once iconic and bizarre, TLC are one of the most unaccountable bands to hit the American mainstream. In the early Nineties, the trio released two provocative albums that somehow managed to connect with mass audiences, even as their strange blend of genres and attitudes went under the radar. They remain one of the most commercially successful female groups of all time, although the challenging impact of their music has yet to be fully understood.

While TLC have received their due for making the link between hip-hop and the Sixties girl group, it's surprising that their style — a unique mix of crudeness and refinement — has not been more influential. This clash in tones represents the diversity of the three members: the late Lisa Lopes, a baby-faced rapper with a penchant for cackling like an old lech; Tionne 'T-Boz' Watkins, a husky alto whose delivery seems to lay down a set of facts; and Rozonda 'Chilli' Thomas, whose youthful voice conveys the sweetness of straight R&B.

Their 1992 debut, *Oooooooohhh... On the TLC Tip*, is a flurry of high spirits and bawdy antics, raucous voices breaking with excitement. The lyrics are sexually uninhibited and wittily allusive, yet these women retain the aura of hopped-up kids, giggling themselves into hysterics. In most of the songs, lewdness is inseparable from a sense of playtime fun; at the same time, a stream of erotic references reminds us that the band is definitely adult.

Two decades on, this album remains as mysterious as ever, with its disorienting shifts of tone. One moment the girls are screeching with laughter, then they're making the crassest of sexual invitations — but when a chorus approaches, their voices rise and become supple and womanly, as Lopes' rapping segues into the harmonies of T-Boz and Chilli. In their bright, baggy clothing, these twenty-something women resemble teenage boys, but part of their posturing is to convince us that, beneath all the armor and androgyny, they have young spirits that need sensitive care.

However, even as they move us with their sweetness, the women are boisterous and uncontrollable. By today's standards, TLC are not particularly suggestive, but they have a way of switching between mature and childish sexuality that is anarchic. The record suggests a world where no boundaries exist between genders and age groups: there is only the energy of willful, hormonally-raging individuals.

On several tracks, the voices of Lopes and T-Boz are so thick that we can imagine their explicit loud mouths, leering at this or that. The three women are like bragging boys who have never been quieted by adolescence — they remain extrovert and overbearing. It's a "craziness" that little girls who are fans of Pink and Bratz dolls might relate to, but taken in a much more idiosyncratic direction. Lopes has a wild laugh that sounds like a teenage snicker, but also the crowing of an old guttersnipe.

It's used to startling effect in the group's breakthrough single, *Ain't 2 Proud 2 Beg*. This signature track, written by Lopes and producer Dallas Austin, is really an extraordinary achievement: it's a mass of conflicting voices set to a huge, complex jive of rhythms. Lopes' voice in this song is both ardent and sniping: she gives us an insider's lowdown, which also has the instructive tone of a sex-ed class. The combination is appropriate for a song about sexual uncertainty: a mix of braggadocio and vulnerability, as well as a plea for the downright horny.

Lopes starts the track with typical swagger, but within seconds, the point of view changes to that of a teenage introvert. The girls chide a society that puts pressure on teens to be sexually active, and the bullying voices that make them feel inadequate. At this point the song appears sympathetic to the introvert, siding with personal convictions over image. Yet as it turns out, peer pressure may be justified: to our surprise, "How can you be happy alone?" is posed as a rhetorical question, as Lopes gears up for an ode to sexual prowess. Could it be that the fear of being an outcast is as good a motivation as any? There is no clear separation between what the speaker wants and what society demands, since the rhythm melds the two together. Then the song rises and what follows is a tremendously hesitating and sensitive bridge, almost maidenly in its yearning ("When I need to feel love... And I want to be touched / And feeling so much.") The loveliness of this melody is unexpected, yet it bubbles up so instinctively that it seems like a logical extension of the previous argument.

Lopes follows up with a posturing speech but, as occurs so often with this artist, a monologue suddenly shifts into multiple voices and is complicated by indecision. She begins with a kind of nonsense didacticism ("Realize the realism of reality"), but at the end of the verse, she switches to a very direct overture: "Yeah, I like it when you [smooching sound] both sets of lips / Ooooooohhh ... on the TLC tip." This has got to be the dirtiest of "oohs," but it also has a little of the disco "ooh" mixed in. The fact that this record packs in so many sounds with specific associations means that each phrase is bursting with possible readings. The songs vocalize and give equal weight to contrary opinions, then interrupt them with odd effects. Lopes combines the sexual inspection common in hip-hop ("Two inches or a yard / Rock hard or if it's saggin'") with a self-effacing gentleness, but in the next moment she flips the tone and does a spoof of girlie behavior.

This album is full of sounds that are both precise and difficult to pinpoint. In *Das Da Way We Like 'Em*, Lopes breaks out into a filthy laugh somewhere between an old man and a witch's cackle. When she utters a sappy line like "I like a man with romance in his heart," she makes a noise so peculiar ("chrk chrk") that it throws off the entire verse. That sound is inexplicable, a little shrieking effect that gives us an internal flutter. We are also distracted by the fact that the intensity of her voice gathers in unusual spots, so that the phrase "takin' a reason, addin' season" turns into a jagged little swirl.

However, even with a motormouth like Lopes up front, the women rely heavily on non-verbal cues and sounds that "speak." The classical harmonies that open *What About Your Friends* are powerful yet turbulent: the resonance of their combined voices suggests a spinning surface, never still. On *This is How It Should be Done*, the title phrase is stretched out so that a quivering belies the assertiveness of the words. As in most TLC songs, the chorus displays a degree of reticence, but just as we're drawn in, that mood is rejigged and overwhelmed by new sounds.

Oooooohhh... On the TLC Tip has a sensational album cover: it shows the three singers in vibrant colors, leaping with joy, like kids in an inflatable castle. Condoms are everywhere, flipping out of belts, but the girls don't seem self-conscious about this. On the back cover, they grin with delight as a strip of bright yellow rubbers juts out from Lopes' shorts. The entire sleeve is a riot of funhouse sexual imagery, with latex peeking out of every available space. The girls wear loose clothing, since their bodies are not on show — far from it. They are swathed in layers, with fluorescent kneepads, and Band Aids are worn as allusions to sexual protection. This luridly colored safety gear draws on a kiddie sense of fun — the pamphlet features childish kisses and scrawls as well as safe-sex messages. The images are a perfect match for the music, openly playing with the connotations of immaturity while dealing in ribald innuendo.

I haven't come across a sleeve that was such a mass of codes to decipher, other than with Prince, but while his notes tend to be presented as the jottings of a Picasso-like genius — and the comparison is justified — there is nothing "masterly" about TLC's presentation. We get the sense of peeking into a very fertile universe, where borders are easily confused. After all, this group has a baby-faced singer with a predilection for cackling like a crone. Even though Lopes' lyrics deal with insecurity, her humor goes recklessly below-the-belt without any concern for balance. Sometimes her voice is infinitely flexible and loose; occasionally, it sounds aged and debauched. Lopes represents a disturbing and perverse sexuality, worked effortlessly into the mainstream.

By their second album, TLC were more polished; *CrazySexyCool* (1994) is a much more professional effort — it doesn't have idiosyncrasies crammed into every verse. However, this album is a showcase for T-Boz as well as Lopes, and as such, it contains as many acts of voice-switching and ventriloquy as their debut. The outstanding *Kick Your Game* is remarkable for its confusion surrounding identity and the ease with which the girls appropriate different voices, attitudes, and genders. Against a thudding bass T-Boz describes the girls' entry into a club, referring to their celebrity when she sings, "All I see is everybody trying to get with me." But when Lopes picks up the story, we gradually realize that she is not singing from her own point of view: instead, she's taking on the role of a starstruck male groupie, who tries to distinguish himself from hangers-on by listing his talents. Lopes serenades herself through the voice of this admirer, while appearing to revert to her "own" position intermittently. She alternates between flattering and rejecting herself; it's hard to tell which character is speaking at any given moment, since this puffed-up courtship is inseparable from the Lopes persona. Throughout the song, the women use similar tones for multiple characters, giving us a dizzying array of viewpoints and mouthpieces, often within the same line.

Creep is probably the "deepest" track on the album, in that it consistently implies depth on a melodic level. T-Boz gives her best voice yet: heavy, low and masculine yet succulent. The harmonies in this track are lovely and curving — we can almost visualize them as arcs sweeping over a bar — but the focus is on T-Boz's brooding, intense vocal, about a woman who reacts to her partner's cheating by having her own affairs, to make up the lack of love. During the verse, her decision is presented as a strong, considered stance, and this is supported by the song's steady pace and the fact that her references to infidelity are also allusions to pitch ("keep it on the down-low"). However, even though T-Boz's delivery is carefully controlled, we can hear that these affairs are taking their toll. The "ooh-ah" of the chorus is full of tenderness; the protagonist may be steadfast, but a voice of pain can't help asserting itself, finally breaking through towards the end. This is a woman who begs not to be anguished and tested further ("Don't mess around with my affection"); she is helpless despite her protestations.

Today, TLC's first two albums seem impossibly complex, filled with contradictory voices that still confound us. Current female artists may be marketed as "crazy," but this tends to be about projecting an image rather than delving into creative chaos. More than ever, performers are compelled to stay on brand, avoiding the paradoxes that might make their work fascinating. By contrast, the video for *Ain't 2 Proud 2 Beg* is full of astounding distortions and contrasts, with its outsize shapes, jabbing gestures and graphic silhouettes. It's as if the usual, art-directed sheen has been peeled away, so that each frame pops violently with color and invention.

Listening to *Oooooooohhh...on the TLC Tip* twenty years later, it's a little dismaying to hear Lopes once again proclaim, "Yeah come on, 1992, TLC kickin' off..." Why didn't music take that leap forward? Why didn't this record become the model for pop rather than the artifact of an amazingly fertile time? TLC embody so many distinctive moods: a sexuality dominated by madness, a world in which hysteria is part of the emotional spectrum of both sexes, the bravado of boys as performed by a band of women, and a particular strain of decadence (conjured by their hoots and yelps) that is theirs alone. The album is like a cauldron, swirling with voices and meanings.

Given a band this overwhelmingly popular, it's essential to make notes on strangeness before ubiquity sets in, especially when we are trying to work out how a song as odd as *Ain't 2 Proud 2 Beg* came into consciousness. The ironization of Eighties and Nineties pop has robbed many songs of their mystery, yet the effects of those tracks are still waiting to be decoded. Which "radical" notions are immediately assimilated — and which ones still stick out? For instance, how did the first strains of Kate Bush come across: was *Wuthering Heights* (1978) uncanny, or was there a part of us, even then, that saw it as "conventionally" quirky? Is the weirdness of Bush — or Lisa Lopes — only apparent in retrospect, or was it visible at the time?

Even if it wasn't for Lopes' death in 2002, there are doubts that TLC's uniqueness could have persisted. *CrazySexyCool* is already much slicker than the stunningly alive debut, while their final albums with Lopes, *FanMail* (1999) and *3D* (2002), are steely-sounding, with little of the group's early elation — they contain hardly any contradictions or craziness.

Most bands are compelling for only a short period of time. Music depends so much on that chance blend of instinct and conviction — the magical intuition that leads the mouth to that precise variation on "ooh." It is now difficult to imagine a time when TLC could have dominated teen pop culture — what kind of strange society would have crowned these women? TLC's debut is one of the last occasions on which I've felt a sense of powerful and unusual associations coming together, and just as fascinating as the record itself is the world it pulls in with it.

TOO SINCERE FOR SCHOOL: TAYLOR SWIFT

My interest in Taylor Swift sparked only in 2014, when she released two head-turning singles. From casual listening over the years, I had dismissed Swift as the prim Juliana Hatfield of our times — possessing strong musicality, but hemmed in by coyness and convention. However, *Blank Space* forced a re-examination, introducing a new character to the world of pop. Its narrator is a baby-faced girl who longs to be unmasked as a horror: Estella and Miss Havisham in one, with full sexual power and malevolence intact. Savoring her beauty as well as her villainy, she offers herself as a poisoned treat to the listener.

As an enchantress, this girl seems to have unlimited powers, listing her own "cherry lips" alongside the other wonders of the world ("crystal skies / I could show you incredible things"). She sounds unassailable, not only because of the lyrics, but due to the intricate vocal and effects, which signal inevitability at every turn. Taylor gives a sweet resonance to "So it's gonna be forever" and then a gorgeous, descending lilt to the phrase "Got a long list of ex-lovers," like a nymph sighing over mortal men. She and collaborator Shellback punctuate each line of the chorus with an "Oh!" — a sound of mock disapproval, as if the same old story is playing out yet again. Then there's the neat little click that pops up whenever Swift sings "blank space, baby," which co-producer Max Martin included precisely because it was "so annoying" — a gotcha sound if there ever was one.

The best sound is the chuckle at the end of the second verse, when Swift cuts to the priceless line: "Baby, I'm a nightmare dressed like a daydream." What a delicious comment on a culture that rewards malice as long as it is accompanied by flawless styling — in this song, you can keep your black heart as long as you conform outwardly. The video shows Swift as a dazzling Daisy Buchanan, leading the male ingénue on a tour of her mansion — although, unlike Daisy, this girl is only too aware that money is the key to her charm. She models an endless parade of outfits, showing off that fun, flirty vibe beloved of Instagram. Despite her tantrums, she remains physically irreproachable, vowing to make you "come back each time you leave" — which the song then fulfills by delivering the chorus once again.

We have already encountered this kind of dark humor in the work of Shakespears Sister — only the effect here is more threatening, given the narrator's girlish sense of privilege, perfectly in tune with the spirit of the times. While Shakespears Sister played aging vamps, *Blank Space* — like most of Swift's later album, *Reputation* (2017) — pairs nastiness with the entitlements of a pert young blonde. If looking like a daydream makes you Teflon, the singer seems determined to push that theory to the limit. How far can cherry lips and blue eyes go in disguising extremes of madness and cruelty? Using her face as carte blanche (with red lipstick for contrast), she takes you through "screaming, crying, perfect storms" and torture. The conceit is that all of this is done for your listening pleasure, since the high, triumphal notes of the chorus come on "you love the game."

It is an exciting moment in pop culture when a woman is this driven towards exposure. Ariana Grande and Britney Spears have toyed with the provocations of being "not that innocent" while remaining safely demure. Swift seems determined to smash through all of that. Like Grande, she has heart-shaped Lolita looks, but she makes them creepy as no other young woman does, foreshadowing the hag behind today's pop star. *Blank Space* shows the perverse sincerity of a girl who loves to trap her man, but can't resist letting him know he's been had. Whatever her faults, moral righteousness isn't one of them: she advertises her beauty as "rose gardens filled with thorns."

With her solidly mainstream image, Swift is less easily marginalized than, say, Cat Power or Fiona Apple. Her looks serve as an alibi, which may be why she refers to them so often. Throughout her career, her lyrics have been preoccupied with her own doll-like quality: rosy cheeks, cute dresses, and those ubiquitous red lips, featured in *Tim McGraw* (2006), *The Moment I Knew* (2012), *Wildest Dreams* (2015), *So It Goes...* (2017), *End Game* (2017), and *I Did Something Bad* (2017). In their fixation on fashion, these songs can sound like excerpts from the play *Love, Loss, and What I Wore*. By describing the same images, in almost the same language every time, Taylor keeps using the one set of flashcards: icons of retro style. It's as if emotion cannot be accessed without the proper visuals in place: what is love without the memory of "that little black dress" and your own blue eyes? In *End Game*, Swift introduces the chorus with the line "here's the truth from my red lips" — even something as wholesome as the truth is never less than varnished. Her lyrics read like product placement for a line of Ralph Lauren-style accessories: always classic and true blue, above trends or diversity.

Swift is as enamored with fashion as Fitzgerald was — and like him, she reveals the money and expertise that go into inspiring the look of love. As for Fitzgerald, glamour may not be everything, but the lack of it is a deal-breaker. In Swift's case, wealth expresses itself in faint pastels, Fifties prep stylings, and the patina of a country club: all the chilling traditions of quality. These effects are part of the stage management in *Blank Space*: the projection of a rich, full life guaranteed to draw in admirers. Unlike some of the other seductive personas in this book — Azealia Banks, Siobhan Fahey, Nicki Minaj — the Taylor of *Blank Space* is no bombshell: she takes a softly-softly approach before whipping out the blade.

That ageless, perhaps sinister, aspect of Americana is addressed in Swift's other indispensable song, *Style* (2014). Once again, Taylor casts herself as the Daisy Buchanan figure, a rich playgirl with a rebel suitor, but this time, both lovers are in on the game. The retro images have hardened into place: each character is a blur of generic styling, from the white T-shirt under his coat to her "good-girl faith and a tight little skirt." Faith is as much part of the package as her outfit — or rather, the *look* of faith is what's needed, to get desire into gear. Religion is made tantalizing, cleansed of its dowdy associations through the cut of a dress. Similarly, even though the guy is said to be a wild-eyed, reckless driver, the couple are in no imminent danger; "wildness" is merely his visual condition, perhaps a hairstyle. He comes complete with "that James Dean daydream look" we all know, while she has "that red lip classic thing that you like." The trading of images at a consumer level has never been more apparent: this couple is literally ready-made for each other, swapping his eyes for her lips, his hair for her clean lifestyle. The chemistry between the pair is undeniable, but their transaction is admirably condensed: I do what works for you, and vice versa. Let's do it — let's fall in love.

Why do images so pedestrian — straight out of the catalogue — seem timeless? Certainly, Taylor never tires of them: "I watch us go round and round each time" suggests a cycle in which the players can be replaced. *Style* begins with the melodrama of a Pat Benatar track — the synth bass creates automatic intensity and the moody vibe of an Eighties teen film — but by the time we reach the chorus, it's clear that this is all spray-on ambience, pre-fab drama. From the brooding potential of the start, the chorus reverts to a strange, mechanical flatness, closing with the brittle repetition of "We never go out of style." The words "James Dean daydream," "long hair, slicked back" and "red lip classic thing" are delivered in icy monotone, as if laying down a series of rules, before giving way to an uplift. The only emotion is the gathering coldness in her voice when she refers to rumors of her man "out and about with some other girl," with the bitter, pointed repetition of "some other girl." However, the guy in this scenario is as much of a "blank space" as most of Swift's male leads: what goes on between the eyes and the hair is anyone's guess, possibly a version of the daydream/nightmare combo we've seen elsewhere.

The song's structure — a sensual buildup that slides into monotone — is exactly matched to its subject. After the turbulence of the opening, Swift sings the chorus with precise, even intonation. We understand that each element, from the lips to the hair, is non-negotiable, part of the overall branding. Like Lana Del Rey, Swift sticks to paper-thin archetypes and a cinematic backdrop, but in Swift's case, the styling is more rigidly enforced. The video for *Style* shows mirrored fragments of eyes and lips, ghostly slivers that get exchanged as part of a real-life romance. "We never go out of style" is less a boast than an assertion of sameness. Love is a game of fashion choices and photogenic angst, with the girl in the dress disappointed once again.

This is a consistent theme in Swift: the notion that once you're in love with a Hollywood prototype, nothing else will do. Her songs are in awe of a commonplace ideal, even if it is one that can be bought. If a girl has "that red lip classic thing that you like," you might find you like it just as well on someone else. The focus is on imagery that remains stupidly deathless over countless iterations.

Swift's music tells us about the *performance* of love. *How You Get the Girl* (2014) walks the listener through the playbook of courtship, showing which scenes need to be acted out, down to the staging of a reunion in the rain. The hero in *I Think He Knows* (2019) is chosen for his "lyrical smile, indigo eyes" and that "boyish look I like in a man" which has the singer thinking like "an architect, I'm drawing up the plans." The narrator of *Love Story* (2008) is a Juliet who offers to write everyone's lines: all a hero has to do is step into the cutout and "just say yes." So many of Swift's lyrics take the form of an insistent scripting, with the singer over-narrating a live situation ("I say...," "Then you say..."), supplying an impossible level of back-story. *Love Story* is hummable but so dense that its lyrics do require memorization (or as *Paste* magazine put it, "once you know the words, it's impossible not to sing along"). It is a strange kind of hit single — both catchy and convoluted, slowed by the character's need to specify every detail of the affair. The chugging line of the chorus implies that the same old romance is playing itself out once again. It portrays a couple whose instincts are unerringly cinematic: their relationship involves hitting the marks and making the right moves. In *Wildest Dreams*, a lover is even complimented on his efficacy in playing to type ("he's so bad but he does it so well").

The pleasure of these songs is in listening to tropes play out, with small variations. The pace of a love story is marked by the signature flash of lipstick, a glance down at a modestly revealing dress; the love interest does not divert too far from James Dean or Montgomery Clift, never approaching the unpredictability of a Brando. When, in *End Game*, Swift sings, "You've been calling my bluff on all my usual tricks / So here's a truth from my red lips," we should know by now that red lips *are* a trick: one of Taylor's finest, since they call attention to her talent for artifice. Swift's lyrics tend to combine preening and pragmatism: her characters have never been afraid to model behaviors simply because they are successful, as in *I Did Something Bad* ("I let them think they saved me ... This is how the world works") and *Blank Space* ("Boys only want love if it's torture / Don't say I didn't, say I didn't warn ya"). With these songs, the explicit message is: I only do this because you like it, and who can argue with that? In this world, what works is a red lip over clean, patrician looks, a pastiche of Fifties good-girl style.

In recent years, Swift has been increasingly upfront about naming and calling out each of her tricks. By *Blank Space*, her beauty has become disturbing: those "cherry lips" seem toxic, all the better to eat you with. In *I Did Something Bad*, a sensation of heat or shame turns out to be a cosmetic effect ("I can feel the flames on my skin / Crimson red paint on my lips"). Whether pouting or smoldering, her characters are very conscious of how they look in love or hate. As a young woman, Swift is happy to toy with freakshow glamour: she can play in the paintbox without ridicule. It's no secret why Taylor values being pretty on the outside, as Courtney Love might say: in today's tabloid culture, looking like a dreamboat is a cover for any kind of motive. Yet Swift has steadily worked on blowing that cover: the album *Reputation* examines the contrast between cuteness and cunning. *Look What You Made Me Do* (2017) shows the bite of steel within that preppy voice. The character in *I Did Something Bad* is a Disney princess with a heart of stone — what is prettiness for, if not a license to act out nightmares? Even as she plays the debutante, Swift is keen to suggest there might be a bad seed inside.

By incorporating fashion and image into her songwriting, Swift has found a way to energize her middlebrow reputation — no easy task, given the unshakeable "basic bitch" meme of the 2010s. Without her gift for style, Swift might risk being the polyester bride of music: her confessional storytelling could be relegated to the dreaded adult-contemporary section. Society has become allergic to the sound of plaint in a woman's voice, dismissing it as whiny privilege or a kind of homespun earnestness. Even an artist as talented as Suzanne Vega has found herself mocked, sidelined as a pop-cultural joke along with Lilith Fair.

Our culture tends to favor work that is archly and deliberately bland (in a word, normcore) over the type of sincerity that Vega projects and which defined Swift's career earlier on. One way to avoid derision as a woman in music is to play the avant-garde game: St Vincent and Alison Goldfrapp are formidable high-art goddesses, closer to installations than performers. Both are critically untouchable, yet they are meticulously high-concept rather than strange.

Swift could never be that cool — her songs are nothing if not accessible. They have the knack of being absolutely tuneful and memorable while making you doubtful of their power — *Blank Space* cheers on a Circe-like witch as she lures her next victim, while *Style* is an unnerving tribute to WASP values. As she ages, Swift may be less carefree about playing the villain — already she has the touch of Miss Havisham about her, the suggestion of a cobwebbed wedding cake. Camille Paglia infamously tagged her as the "Nazi Barbie" of pop, wielding her red lips and white skin as a weapon. But no-one has taken this much pleasure in smashing decorous ideals: exposing identity as a mask, building up the façade only to tear it down. And she does it all with such gusto! One thing's for sure: the baby doll has teeth.

SADE IS THE PERFECT PEACH

A taste of Sade is like biting into choice fruit: all sweet spot and exact mellowness, going down easy. Sade has none of the stridency, the bitter tang, of the other artists in this book. Rather than a particular genre of beauty, her voice conjures *the* romantic ideal — the red rose, the ripe peach, the central motifs of love. Her voice is mysteriously edgeless, like slipping into a warm bath: instant lushness, with no pushback. She is never in danger of belting or sounding stroppy, because her voice doesn't seem to pierce the air.

It's a mystique that has drawn an unusual group of male fans, including Mike Patton, Jay-Z, Snoop Dogg, Lil Wayne, Talib Kweli, and Kanye West. Artists with hardcore values are prepared to make her their one exception: a dream of class and fragile perfection. Why her? Sade's voice is never less than alluring, especially when describing being hurt. Her signature songs are masochistic, recalling lost bliss or pain at the hands of yet another cad, the "Western male" who figures so strongly in her imagination. Through it all she remains subdued, somewhat passive for one who has been injured, but there is always something to keep the ear coming back.

A possible comparison might be with Ella Fitzgerald — another supple, yielding voice, equally fluent in depicting pleasure or pain — but Ella never came across as a specific character: her sound seemed to represent the spirit of the times more than any one person. When Bing Crosby declared that "Man, woman or child, Ella is the greatest of them all," he drew attention to the ageless, genderless quality of her persona. Ella's voice was inhumanly flexible, which allowed her to smooth over the strangeness of Cole Porter's lyrics without causing alarm. We don't hear her relishing a particular word or favoring one sound over another — in fact, it's hard to picture a body outside the set of pipes. Another singer might get stuck repeating "Plymouth Rock" three times in a verse, but Ella keeps gliding through: she doesn't have the persistent, haunting tics that a more limited vocalist might show.

Sade does get stuck — and it creates the most compelling moments in her music. Amidst the flow of her voice, what we wait for are the notes of tension and brittleness: the plosives that burst in the earphones, the hard crack of a consonant cutting into all that lush smoothness. Her best-known hit, *Smooth Operator* (1984), portrays a woman seduced by a rogue who flies "coast to coast, LA to Chicago," the "classic case" of a double-crosser. Sade is British and the video is clearly set in a London club, with a local spiv as her love interest, so why the references to America? Listing the man's travels allows Sade to delve into a series of rich "c" sounds, particularly the ones in "Chicago." Coddling each "c," she works up a savory thickness in her mouth — a sensation that dominates the track. As such, this is less a song about despair than a chance to luxuriate in splendor, to gargle words like "Key Largo" in one's throat. Sade's accent is plummy (as in both posh and salivating), and she gets every last drop of juice out of each phrase.

Although she tends to play betrayed women, the fact is that Sade is a decadent — a singer who enjoys "tasting" every sound, lolling a word around like hard candy. What's memorable in *Smooth Operator* is not the rather generic story of deception, but the thick-cut "c" sounds and the hint of a punk gasp on "no need to ask." Her style encourages us to dwell on the formation of words more than their meaning: we have an unusual awareness of what she must be doing with her teeth and tongue at any given time. Sade gets hooked on luxe mouth movement, to the point where the primary aim of the songs appears to be getting variations on texture, rather than lyrical or melodic originality.

To that end, *Kiss of Life* (1992) may be Sade's most successful track, in that our attention is firmly fixed on every change in timbre, from grainy to silky, seamless to cracked. No need to ask if the lyrics are banal: the only notable words refer to the singer's tone, such as asking "Wasn't it clear from the start?" when her own voice is miraculously pure. The song is full of little plays on texture and affect: she sensuously slurs a phrase, then repeats it cleanly and deliberately — "kissolai" is followed by an emphatic "kiss of life," "gimmelumye" is revealed to be "giving me love, yeah."

Sade does this again and again, not only in *Kiss of Life*, but in many of her singles: *Hang On to Your Love* (1984), *Never as Good as the First Time* (1986), and *Smooth Operator*. She alternates between a drowsy murmur and fastidiously neat pronunciation, so that what we remember is the cut-out clarity of the phrase rather than its meaning. When the impact of her voice is carefully measured out, we become conscious of the even spacing between words. You know how quilting a piece of silk enhances its richness, by creating a series of tender buttons? This is what Sade does with her enunciation: she makes cuts into that deep, luscious texture, so that each word becomes a succulent morsel.

Sade has largely been ignored by critics, for the reason that her lyrics exclusively describe love and loss. She sings within her small comfort zone, either in ecstasy or post-pain numbness, sticking to the same range and low-tempo grooves. For the *Guardian's* Alexis Petridis, it's "the sort of music that middle managers from the sticks put on in the background when they think they're going to get their leg over." But something odd is at work when a singer seems indifferent to subject, putting all her focus into the delectation of each syllable. I'm reminded of linguist Geoff Nunberg's comments on the phrase "cellar door," said to be the most beautiful in English despite its semantic banality. For Nunberg, the phrase is "an occasion ... to discern beauty in the names of prosaic things," to strip language "down to its pristine phonetic bones." Sade's lyrics might be the equivalent of "cellar door": all soft, liquid sounds under the guise of rote expression.

Choosing lyrics for their mellifluous potential is unlikely to start trends or find acclaim, no matter how gorgeous or wine-dark the results. Sade gives the best husk, the best whisper, and the coolest clarity, but no-one gives out awards for timbre — in the age of *The Voice* and *American Idol*, pop is all about melisma and hitting the money notes. While I can't necessarily remember what her songs are "about," each application of texture is striking and meticulous — lisping to give some wet sheen to a word, waving the mic around to cloud up the sound. In *Kiss of Life*, we envision the way that her lips must have curved to get that gauzy wraparound effect.

In a wonderful 2014 essay for *Pitchfork*, the American critic Mike Powell proposed a new model for music criticism:

Ultimately the way we talk about music doesn't come down to prescribed terms, but associations, poetics, and the way language has the potential to open music up rather than shut it down. I remember a friend once telling me that a song sounded like braids to her, as in hair. This wasn't just an unusual thing to say about music, but an observation that tapped into this particular song's dense, overlapping rhythmic structure without deferring to words like "syncopation" or "staccato." A few more riffs on the braid metaphor and you'd have what I'd call an insight: A statement that takes something you thought you already understood and makes you see it in a new way.

We need more "braid" writing on music, attempts to discuss the feel and tone of songs without using technical terms and jargon, or placing the work in a socio-historical context. A voice like Sade's demands an analysis beyond genre and background, since her biography, orthodox lyrics, and conventional use of jazz tropes tell us nothing about her influence. Instead, she treats every phrase as if it were "cellar door," liaising her words Parisian-style and then breaking them up, for maximum sensuous effect.

Movie directors know that if we are going to invest ourselves in a world, we want to be enveloped by sound as much as vision. If we see a scene in New York, we need to hear the rush of the subway and the click of hard heels on pavement in order to feel immersed. In a high-end film, a sense of luxury comes from the thick sounds of glassware and silver as much as the images. Certain noises are the audio equivalent of eye candy: the clean sound of folding a newspaper, an apple being sliced, the satisfying splodge of a dollop of cream.

Sade appeals to listeners on that level: the part of us that thrills to hearing pure notes juxtaposed with raspy sounds, a razor slitting though plush softness, or a purr that makes one's entire body stand to attention. Her voice unlocks the hidden synesthesia in all of us.

IT'S FOR YOUR BODY:
CHAKA KHAN'S INTERNAL RHYTHMS

Given the chance, this music will take you over — we know that from the way it unravels. Chaka Khan and Rufus' *Ain't Nobody* (1983) begins with a tiny keyboard loop: it turns and twists, unwrapping and expanding as it goes. It is the kind of percolating sound you hear in documentaries about the beginnings of life, where music pulses as we see an organism grow and germinate. As the loop gets louder, we can't help but take on its momentum, waiting for an imminent leap.

Chaka Khan's voice is about the freeing of energy: the ability to make a sound that releases the tension of all that coiling and uncoiling. Yet the climaxes of her songs lie in unexpected places. Instead of launching a gymnastic high note — like most of the contestants on *The Voice* — Khan's outburst draws on the vibrating strength of the whole body. The peak of *Ain't Nobody* is a series of mounting breaths ("oh-oh-oh-ohhh"): the first three ascend, while the final "oh" floats slightly down, as if light-headed from all the exhalation. These "ohs" are not particularly urgent or forceful — they merely give us the sublime sense of being buffeted upwards, by a series of feather-light strokes. Taking that last breath imparts a deep sense of satisfaction: the shoulders instantly drop, the body relents. It's the antithesis of the pressure required to sustain a virtuoso note.

This is one of the greatest "ohs" in R&B — which is saying something when you consider that here is a genre based on drawing out sensation, finding opportunities and pretexts for the utterance of "oh," in all its glorious variations. But crucially, Khan's cry is only the manifestation of an energy that has been building throughout the song. Its lead-in is a bridge where the singer hopes that "this night will last forever," so that "oh-oh-oh" becomes a gliding continuation of the word "forever." "Oh" is all of a piece with the rest of the song, with the same timbre and soft focus of the verse.

This is possible because Khan's is a miraculous voice, which keeps its warmth and matte tones at any pitch, any volume: it maintains a very slight smoke, the texture of brushed copper. Her self-described "bumblebee" vibrato is a sensuous, fibrous sound that all but guarantees a bodily reaction: the prick of fine hairs through the skin. Eighties funk may not be the most respectable of genres, but look who's shivering! The title of another Khan hit, *Do You Love What You Feel* (a rhetorical statement — no question mark), may well be the singer's ethos. Sensation comes first: the classification of love can wait.

Instinct and spontaneity — the idea that the body knows best — are lyrical conceits throughout Khan's work. *Ain't Nobody*[1] speaks of a feeling "captured effortlessly," while the heroine of *I'm Every Woman* (1978) claims that her powers are all intuitive ("Anything you want done, baby / I'll do it naturally"). But the subject of naturalness is best conveyed in musical terms. In *Ain't Nobody*, the elemental bubbling of the intro creates the feeling that the melody is moving where it wants to. The spiraling synth suggests an organism evolving and doubling, readying us for the space-expansion of the vocal. Khan's voice has a bio-acoustic

---

1 There's a reason why double negatives work so well in song titles: *Ain't Nobody, Ain't No Sunshine, (I Can't Get No) Satisfaction*. They allow the singer to be slangy and emphatic, but also defiantly illogical: the negatives don't cancel each other out, so that the "redundant" one exists purely for reasons of rhythm.

quality, the ability to suggest pulsing and breathing in its undulations. This is a song made of breath: the gentle whir of the voice and synth working together, the flying "ohs" that bear us off towards the chorus. Yet even at its most ethereal, the vocal retains a physical intimacy — it slides right into the body's comfort zone.

I'm Every Woman gives further insight into Khan's powers, with its references to spell-casting and clairvoyance. This song has become such a standard that its basic weirdness is easy to overlook. Early on, the singer lets us know that she is essentially a deity, all-conquering and omniscient: "I can read your thoughts right now, every one from A to Z." We might expect some sort of fireworks here, but instead the psychic revelation turns out to be a series of sounds: "Whoa, whoa, whoa." What kind of mind-reading is this? Instead of putting on a display, Khan chooses to turn inwards — her assurance leads us to believe that "whoa" says it all. These inner soundings, deep and sonorous, contain everything we need to know (or at least, as much as she will tell us).

The video shows several Chakas singing these "divining" sounds, while a black-clad Chaka responds with a further, reflective series of "whoas." Though their meaning is unclear, the effect of these echoes is hypnotic. As the vibrating cries fold into one another, they create a rich blur of sound — the interplay suggests that Khan is listening to her own performance, weaving her comments into the existing melody. The wall of "whoa" dominates the song — the fact that it is offered as proof of supremacy, literally absorbing and silencing all questions of logic, shows the respect accorded to non-verbal sounds in R&B. In this track they are not shout-outs, but expressions of underlying rhythm, like reverberations from within an instrument. It's hard to think of a more full-bodied sound — it warms both the belly and the tongue as you sing it, especially in the context of nourishing lyrics ("It's all in me.").

For this reason, *I'm Every Woman* is self-reflexive. When Khan talks of her magical intuition, we think of her ability to transmit emotional affect within every nuance of this song: through a slight extension of the tongue, making a cushion of her mouth, or by sensually muffling the sound in the manner of a brass instrument. So much of R&B is about the precise infusion of the "oh," the plenitude of the "whoa" — and this "whoa" in particular requires the lower lip to get supple. Lyrics can be sung to awaken muscle memory as much as anything else: as in The Beatles' *Come Together* (1969), where the words "juju," "mojo," and "toe-jam" are merely signifiers of funk — pretexts to juice up the mouth. In funk, blues-rock, and disco, that impulse to plump up the sound makes the difference between a serviceable track and a great one.

Khan's third signature track, *I Feel for You* (1984), was written and recorded by Prince five years earlier — his version is a wonderful work in its own right, but what Prince's take doesn't have is the full, blooming sensuality of Khan's voice, Stevie Wonder's harmonica, or the infamous "Chaka Khan" rap by Grandmaster Melle Mel. Producer Arif Mardin[2] has Mel open the song by stuttering the singer's name over and over ("Chaka, Chaka, Chaka, Chaka Khan, Chaka Khan"), knocking all the "ch" and "k" sounds together to get a good friction going, and then proceeding to riff on that effect ("Chaka Khan, let me rock you / Let

---

2 The stuttering of Chaka's name occurred when Mardin's hand accidentally slipped on the repeat machine, creating a percussive effect he decided to work with. This is the kind of felicity that makes a song truly memorable, and which record companies can't bank on getting in the studio: like chemistry or screwball timing, it can't be pre-programmed. A happy accident is more likely to take place during relaxed rehearsal, with time for improvisation and camaraderie between producers and performers — all the elements squeezed out of the current pop industry.

me rock you, Chaka Khan"). Gargling these rich, chocolatey sounds primes us to savor sensation, very much in the style of a Gertrude Stein poem. (Would Bowie's *Changes*, 1971, be as great without all the static electricity of the "ch-ch-ch-ch" to make the word stand up and bristle, rather than lying flat?[3]) Along with the scratched records on the turntable, Melle Mel's intro works up the heat necessary to get the song into gear — it also lets us know what a uniquely tactile track this will be.

After the "chaka" locomotive,[4], Khan's voice comes floating in, light and hazy, telling us that when it comes to love, "it's mainly a physical thing." The chorus contains only two lines, "I feel for you" and "I think I love you," surrounded by so much air and space that they might blow right over us. It becomes apparent that the title has a different meaning from the one on paper — "I feel for you" doesn't refer to empathy, the way it would if written or spoken. When Khan presses on the word "feel," the focus is on sensation and pulling power, the ability to fully immerse the listener (in the video, she draws great handfuls of air towards her, enhancing the feeling of plunge). Unlike sympathy or identification, this is a feeling that is "mainly physical" — almost graspable, given the textural impressions we're getting. "Feel" works similarly to the "whoa" from *I'm Every Woman* — it relays a specific affect through sound, with Khan's voice seeming to get closer and hotter as she utters the word.

---

3 In pop lyrics, stammering is a way to give strain and awkwardness to a phrase that might sound overly cool or pat. The protagonists of Bowie's *Changes* and Talking Heads' *Psycho Killer* (1977) turn smooth talk into a stuttering hot mess.

4 The hustling "chaka" of *I Feel for You* anticipates the "ch-ka" of Yello's *Oh Yeah* (1985) — one of the most precise "nonsense" sounds in pop, with its click-on, click-off effect.

It's no coincidence that Khan is at her best with songs that refer to bodily changes — in *I'm Every Woman* she offers to "mix a special brew, put fire inside of you," while *I Feel for You* is about tapping into the "warm feelin' inside." It is the "gladdening" of her voice[5] — the way it develops a warm sheen as it moves over a single word – that makes it so distinctive. This is the haptic effect of Chaka Khan: the sense of her music applying vibrations to the body, like a cat rubbing up against you. There is the illusion of absolute surround sound, a feeling we get from the toes up rather than the head down, in contrast to the model of the literate singer/songwriter. Khan's voice implies a curious forward motion, as if expressing the melody's own yearning — when a B wants to go up to a C. When she leans on a word like "feel" or "love," the music itself seems desirous — notes bend towards each other, indicating a fond dependence.[6]

---

5 "Gladdening" moments, as I term them, are most often found in funk, soul, and especially Quiet Storm, the mellow African American genre prominent in the 1970s and 1980s. Today, popular music doesn't seem to crave that swoonsome sound, filing it under the dreaded adult-contemporary section along with the mature love duet. However, a more recent example of this kind of soulful insinuation can be heard in Estelle and Kanye West's *American Boy* (2008), a hip-hop take on transatlantic relations. When Kanye, in a rap that is both bragging and insightful, tells us he feels like "Mike at his *bad*-dest / Like the Pips at their *glad*-dest," he not only salutes two greats, but performs that excessive *lean* which is characteristic of Philadelphia soul. In turn, Estelle stretches out her lines ("walking that *walk*"), giving them a lingering tail-off, an effect that the video reproduces by elongating her shadow. Estelle has a wonderful habit of tapering off her notes so that they threaten to go off-key: the result is that the first flavor of the sound is different from its aftertaste.

6 This clinging attachment between notes can also be achieved through lyrics. In *Let's Do It, Let's Fall in Love* (1928), Cole Porter uses the phrase "Lithuanians and Letts do it" to give an extra push

Khan can let a phrase suggestively trail off, like a curve towards an asymptote. As we know from Janet Jackson, sounds can be just as shamelessly insinuating as words (which might bring up the concept of "slutty" music), and these vibrations stroke us, with the insistent nuzzling of an animal.

In the world of stand-up, there is a distinction made between the comedian who "says funny things" and the one who "says things funny." It's the difference between Tina Fey and Kristen Wiig: the smart person whose soundbites work just as well in print, versus the actor who can make each line personally hers, inseparable from her unique phrasing and gestures. Chaka Khan is clearly the latter, a performer who can "say things" sexy, louche, funny or any way she wants, in tones that imprint themselves on the listener. Each "whoa" in *I'm Every Woman* is irreplaceable, making us internalize the physical memory of that cry, the inhalations it took to get there. Khan energizes the conceit of feeling like a natural woman, with the intensely fleshy sound of her voice and the love-shaping of each syllable.

It is the mark of the greatest songs that they can mysteriously enact what they describe. In the dance classic *Gypsy Woman* (1991), for instance, singer Crystal Waters not only tells us about neglect but evokes it through the parched, meager quality of her voice — a strange sound we shrink from.[7] Khan can embody just about anything she

---

to the next iteration of "let's do it." As a result, "let's" is pronounced as if italicized — it becomes more adhesive, as if reluctant to peel off from the rest of the line. This is appropriate for a song about the involuntary slide towards one's base instincts.

7 The American house singer Crystal Waters has one of the most curious timbres: like a voice heard from afar, with an overlay of drone. The subject of her great hit *Gypsy Woman* is a homeless person, but even before we realize this, there is something worn and bedraggled about her delivery. Hearing that nagging, faded

names — her voice slinks across like a caress when it refers to desire, a movement descriptive of the female body. Just as a guitarist can use a talkbox to "vocalize" notes (most notoriously in Bon Jovi's *Livin' on a Prayer*, 1986, where it functions as a sonic hand puppet), Khan's cries have a "speaking" quality — they are as explicit as one can get without verbal communication.

But Chaka is still underappreciated — we don't hear her routinely mentioned among the first rank of singers, along with Aretha or Etta or even Adele. Part of this may be her association with disco and danceability: there may be the feeling that something so infectious precludes greatness. Today, disco riffs are most often heard as samples, isolated and truncated so that there is no risk of music overtaking the senses. They exist as pockets of lushness in a sparse, linear setting à la Daft Punk — a band who specialize in distilling disco for contemporary tastes. Irresistibly upbeat tunes are scarce, unless they come in the ironically weak and watered-down form of a Nouvelle Vague or from a patently retro act like Bruno Mars.

Disco is not seen as canonical in the same sense as blues or rock, with the exception of Giorgio Moroder's precise

---

voice pulled over endless dance beats unsettles us, more than any bitter lyric could. Obvious black humor would only dilute the effect of the aural paradox: the fact that the singer invites empathy for the homeless even though her own voice is tense and ungiving, clearly going through the motions. In most of her singles, Waters manages to sound both harsh and lifeless, mechanically expressing desire ("I want ya ... I want ya") or pleasure ("Makin' happy, makin' happy, happy, happy, happy"). Waters, like Sade and Rihanna, has a distinct reserve and inscrutability in her voice: a quality that is underrated. Today's acclaimed vocalists, such as Adele, seem to favor classic belting and a direct line to the emotions, conspicuously giving it their all, but I contend that a great voice needs strangeness in its tone: some element that is difficult to process.

soundscapes and the ultra-lean stylings of Nile Rodgers. Against such crystalline perfection, Chaka Khan's voice and music can seem like an embarrassment of riches: overripe and in need of tamping down. We live in times of low tolerance for unbridled pop exuberance — the sumptuous emotionalism and womanliness of many disco classics can read as dated. Add to this a lack of obvious verbal showmanship (the lyrics tend to draw from doo-wop's legacy of powerful "nonsense" sounds), and it's no surprise that this is the most maligned of genres.

But disco was never the inane search for thrills its detractors made out — for the most part, it comes by its euphoria honorably. Think of Michael Jackson's single *Off the Wall* (1980), and the way its utopian nightlife is never far from a dreary, routine existence: the "nine to five" and the need to believe that "life ain't so bad at all." When was the last time you heard a song discuss decadence in relation to the stresses of the working week? Disco is just as interested in the bridge-and-tunnel crowd as the fashion elite — maybe more, since its sublime visions stand in greater contrast to a shabby life.

The fantasy offered by disco was in fact its promise of endlessness: that while the beat continues, there will be no comedown. The lyrics are often tongue-twisters, designed to revolve in the mouth as the rhythms twist the hips, creating a perpetual motion machine. We can hear this spiral movement in the regenerative loop that opens *Ain't Nobody*, and in the multiple Chakas who spin through *I'm Every Woman*. Perhaps the best-known example of the "forever" sound in disco is in Cheryl Lynn's *Got to Be Real* (1978), where the word "re-ea-ea-ea-l" is stretched to breaking point, like an ever-extending hose. While keeping a mundane reality in view, disco promotes a whirl without end: through a supernaturally flexible voice, a wall of orchestration, and the inexhaustible permutations of the synth. The projected center of every dancefloor is the boundless happiness released by the wild, wanton vocals of a Chaka Khan.

Disco confuses the body by replacing the heartbeat with a frantic pulse, and using ascending patterns to imply heat and acceleration. In a similar way, Khan blurs the line between haptic and audio, her voice giving off vibrations you swear you could touch or taste. Too often, the tactile and imagistic effects of music are written off as subjective or fanciful, an excuse for over-writing. But science has already shown that sound can reverse the evidence of our other senses: imparting a fresh crunch to stale food, making cold water feel warm, or faking the taste of cream in black coffee. The latter tells us something about the thickening and cooling effect of sound — the ability to seem so luscious that even the tongue is fooled. The right sound can cause us to experience a sensation as hard or soft, close or distant, bitter or tangy.

While we await further experiments, listen to Chaka's three deathless songs — this is music that loves what it feels. Notice how we're given time to absorb the charge of "whoa, whoa, whoa," the cooling-off period that follows the heated "I think I love you," and the way the depression of the word "feel" makes it a tender button. On the evidence of the body, the sensation is real.

ALL THOSE ANOMALIES:
AZEALIA BANKS FEAT. NICKI MINAJ AND RIHANNA

Romantic Futures: Azealia Banks

Azealia, Rihanna, Nicki: these women are the greatest gifts to bowerbirds and magpies around the world, with their instinctive collection of the diverse. Pulling from all sources, time periods, and regions — from Cockney England to France to ancient Greece, from Barbados to Jamaica to Trinidad — they save up every scrap of sound they have ever heard, investing these fragments with epic pulling power.

None of the fused girls possess a single voice: they are most "themselves" when they speak in multiple tongues, confusing the cadence of one language with the structures of another. Their lyrics are full of hybrid words, seemingly coined on impulse, as well as non-lexical sounds that are strangely attractive: hard to transcribe, but somehow easy on the ear. Any attempts at "coherence" would be less than authentic, a betrayal of the values these women are committed to: the fully lived, impure nature of their ideals.

Azealia Banks, the Euro-sophisticate rapper from New York, has assured us that she is both a mermaid and the inheritor to Poseidon's throne; in truth, she is closer to a gorgon or hydra, with her flashing eyes and writhing serpentine body. Faces that are both hard and sexualized produce a special kind of apprehension, and Azealia has wicked, shocking eyes: bright, blank, depthless. Despite having all the features of conventional beauty, this woman has made herself loathsome to look at.

While her eyes transfix us, Azealia keeps running her mouth off, throwing out a series of rhymes at furious speed. Each of these raps is a network of interlaced voices, crammed with archetypes both familiar and newly formed. These words are so tightly stitched that it is hard to distinguish between universal and personalized imagery, since references to Aphrodite and Isis are mashed into a descriptor like "porcelain-Snowflakin' Papi." Her rat-a-tat-tat delivery means that singular expressions are tossed off with the ease of a cliché, from a boast ("young kill-em-in-the-denims") to a strident yet puzzling declaration ("I be in that prissy stone set," "I be looking very heavy metal and reflective"). The fast flow is impossible to duplicate, leaving us gasping her in her wake.

Video directors love to zoom in on Azealia's motormouth, cutting between its moves and slo-mo erotic shots of her body. The effect is disorienting, drawing out the lag between her description of an image and our ability to picture it. It is challenging to keep up with the whiplash changes of perspective between and even within lines, since Azealia morphs between "I," "you," and "her" — the latter an aloof, desirable commodity, no longer accessible to the protagonist. Sometimes she spits bile at a bitch, but just as often she is that "elite rap bitch" herself, embracing all the hateful qualities of hardness.

Part of what makes Azealia such a sure-shot is her use of onomatopoeia. Sounds like "pitty-pat-pat-pat" imitate the sharp clip of gunfire, giving the impression of unstoppable acceleration. Azealia is fond of small, sharp repetitions; two words that click together like maracas. "Clock clock," "dip dip," and "bang bang" are clearly used as counters, but so are "skate straight" and "spit slick." Then there are the unexpected inversions ("hip pop," "Cola Coca") that create a delayed click, and the non-verbal sounds ("yizzap-yap" and "click-clazzack clack") that are straight-out crazed.

Somehow the tongue never gets mangled in all these twists and turns, even when it comes to avant-garde levels of poetry. The lyrics for 2014's *Desperado* ("Ups and ups, seductive pup," "Mutts in tux, deluxe and such") conjure swank and status in such elliptical terms that one is reminded of Pavement's Stephen Malkmus, and his ability to build mood out of non sequiturs. But did Malkmus ever sketch elegance with such relaxation and lightness ("Attire, tea, a style / Look how ya looking now!" from *Miss Camaraderie,* 2014)? Rapping at top speed makes Azealia's verbal ingenuity seem offhand; even the offer of "cheddar, chinchilla, feathers and leathers" in *Jumanji* (2012) hardly surprises us. It is an assortment of objects by texture and rhyme, giving us words and ideas to chew on.

Azealia's lyrics are a nonsense buffet of language. Although her rapid-fire lines allow few points of entry, out of that toxic mouth comes a lush fruit from time to time. Cherries and plums are often mentioned — most notoriously in her signature track, *212* (2011), where "Now she wanna lick my plum in the evenin'" offers a rhyme with "I guess that cunt getting eaten." But unlike most speakers (in music and society), Azealia pronounces "cunt" with lip-smacking complacency rather than anger. There is such an overflow of desire and appetite in these tracks: the singer is a rapacious eater, keen to taste every word in the world. In the gorgeous track *Luxury* (2012), Azealia goes all out, giving a sensuous, sloppy-mouthed vocal. The extruded words of the chorus ("Your l-l-l-love, my L-U-X-U-R-aye ya know what I would") are an excuse to ladle attention over every syllable, with the lavish delectation of each "l" sound. In the video, Azealia's high-gloss lips — a visual correlative for her voice, along with her rampant tongue-flipping — show that the song is really about the pleasures of timbre and language, overwhelming any message of love to the listener.

For Azealia, everything is food: every texture, even the taste of metal, can be made luscious and expensive. In *Heavy Metal and Reflective* (2014), a striking early line ("I be very freaky tickled cherry") sets us up to savor the title later on ("I be looking very heavy metal and reflective"). Azealia is clearly one artist who has not given up on lyrical originality, inviting us to dwell on her compelling and curious wording. Language is meat and drink to her, which means that anything is edible, including bodies ("Denim and a satin rump / Blend it with the carrot blush," from *Desperado*). Even food needs to eat in order to sate itself — as we hear in the track *1991* (2012), "Cocoa want the cream in abundance." The gratuitous references to meals and wealth are about a dense pile-up of textures, giving you numerous variations on feel and taste. In *Ice Princess* (2015), Azealia finds a hundred ways to make you crave coldness, from "These glaciers glamour and glisten" and "Igloo'd, cold-cased and bodied" to "Corrosive, the coldest, city is a tundra / Stay focused, no wonder, frigid princess come from."

This is an artist for whom money is bread and cheddar, for whom pleasure is cream and dripping honey. Some of the most thrilling moments occur when Azealia describes her lust for chocolate, sweetmeats, and any number of the fresh fruity sodas she enjoys. On *Desperado*, she even invents a new flavor ("I be Aquafizzy or that Passion Punch/ Or the fashion's munch but the fabric's lush") — is Aquafizzy the preferred drink of mermaids? And her celebration of effervescence in *Soda* (2014) captures the intoxication of sensual pleasure. Did the Beats write a better tribute to Americana than "Icy Cola Coca, Sprite I love the most-a! / I ride rollercoasters! I try all the cultures!" Or: "I say soda, soda? / Tie-dye o'er / I roll the dice / I coast! I dose!" Gertrude Stein would have loved the million-dollar question from *Yung Rapunxel* (2014): "Who was fooding this fish?"

No-one enjoys "fooding" more than Azealia, but for all that, it is words that are luxury and abundance, even more than the tastes they describe. Listen to her rapping "bitches zooted and sipped / I'm suited and zipped," and notice the luxe feeling we get as words slip out of their covers and get sewn into new ones. Azealia pronounces certain words with as much relish as if they were juicy goodies. Consider, for instance, her odd attraction to the term "bezel": a word that provides a partial rhyme with her own name, as well as signifying fabulous antique riches, a refined upgrade from bling. "If the fifth pop, pray for your butter" is a yummy mouthful more than a warning, smacking of roasted corn. And who can resist this gracious, if baffling, invitation from *JFK* (2014): "Do you dine or tea, Italian for two?" It is a line that maintains impeccable surface manners and deference, without the need for content.

In the chorus for *Treasure Island* (2018), the singer dotes on a word of her own invention: "pleasuries," which evokes a cornucopia of delights, more than mere "pleasure" would. It sounds like a term coined by John Donne, in order to seduce. Choruses are where Azealia moves into her siren self, a relief from the blaring and obscenity of the verses. On the refrains of *Luxury, Liquorice* (2011), *Miss Amor* (2014), *Miss Camaraderie*, and *The Big Big Beat* (2016), she speaks the language of love, combing her hair while enticing men onto the rocks. This sweet, melodic Azealia seems eager to please, addressing the listener as "sir," "mister" or "monsieur," and asking to be his pidgin sweetheart. The treats she dangles in *Treasure Island* include "my little sex face, wanna see what it look like," and this impressive postcard: "Picture me on a jet ski, the pick of the litter."

In *Miss Amor*, she gives out a delirious (if generic) series of love tokens in the chorus ("Pure, lovely allure / A lovely

Aurora, monsieur my eyes are wide ... oh see my heart"),
professing the innocence she never shows in verses. This
is not the queer, mischievous Azealia of *212*, but a woman
offering a man all the "pleasuries" of the world, pleasury
being a unit of hedonism. However, we know that she can
revert to the scheming Azealia at any moment; another
line ("Mod-dern witch I are / Delightful Miss Amor, señor,
señor!") hints that sorcery is afoot.

As with her attraction to food, Azealia's use of myth is
a way of casting herself as a sensualist for the ages. Along
with a litany of boasts and grudges, the songs abound with
references to classical idylls: the blue bay, the azure (if not
wine-dark) sea, models of stately perfection. With these
descriptions of paradise, the singer makes a cool claim
on all of world mythology: Greek and Roman gods, the
book of fairytales, the American Western, not to mention
the sweetest confections pop culture has to offer. If there
is anything unusual about a young black woman taking
ownership of this territory — claiming direct descendance
from mermaids, Aurora, and the lost city of Atlantis — then
Azealia doesn't know it. Not content with the usual riches
flaunted by rappers, she is a pioneer in terms of viewing
the whole universe as part of her cultural inheritance.
Quite casually, she adopts a world picture as her personal
backdrop (as she explains in *Atlantis*, 2012, "I took the
blue out the sea and put the blue in the weave"). Azealia
places herself dead center: at the heart of mythology, never
marginalized.

Even though the singer admits that the microgenre of
seapunk "is a joke ... not a real thing," she is happy to ride the
wave of her creation myth, making consistent references to
herself as an aquatic goddess, and driving up momentum
using the power of water ("Hydro, whipping, counting,
crowning"). New York is her raised Atlantis: rediscovered as
the city of lore, this time with her installed as its sovereign.

1991 sees Azealia challenging the ruling class, brandishing her youthful flexibility ("Young kill-em-in-the-denims / Young venom on the M-I-C / Young villain"). She describes herself as fearsome, toxic, and super-hot — but above all as young, with unlimited powers of verbal flow. As the fastest spinner around, she will usurp the staid king and queen.

On *ATM Jam* (2013), Azealia is the ultimate jetset traveler, living the *"bonne vie"* (and not the more common *dolce vita*) while flitting between continental and American accents. She starts with a parody of an English party girl, then suddenly gives a rich Spanish trill to "rrrrip-pap" as if saying "Ay caramba!" Describing her penchant for fusing two unlikely words, Azealia christens herself a "hyphy hip-cat," and then something else that's feline and European: a "high-sophisti-chat," the toast of international society. Though New York-born and bred, the rapper's persona is based on a fluency in foreign cultures and mythology, demonstrating a mastery — and effortless mixing — of tongues.

This is not so incongruous when you consider that Azealia has branded the rudiments of words and culture as her own personal trademarks. Referencing the stunning impact of her debut track *212* — the shot heard round the world — she drops the signature "1-2" throughout her records, as a reminder of her authority. Another signature is her initials, "A-B," emblazoned over multiple songs as a designer logo ("Look at pretty A-B / Pretty A-B, pretty pretty A-B / Damn, little bam" from *Van Vogue*, 2012), and as a fundamental binary code ("A-B, A-B, the two letters" in *Jumanji*).

What keeps Azealia from further success is her habit of being a provocative, sometimes vicious, loudmouth on social media, flinging out bait on topics from Trump to skin-bleaching. Her desire to play the villain is incorrigible — even outside her music, she casts herself as the abject

Azealia, spraying venom and rage. But whether or not she flames out early, there is no denying she is a pistol: the most formidable female rapper we have had since Neneh Cherry. She has an entitlement that simply assumes ownership of past and present, with a view to future domination. The fact that Azealia has patented the double click of "1-2" and "A-B" as an activation of her sound shows the scope of her ambitions. If you can claim the building blocks of language as your own, then surely the world is yours.

Cool as Sphinx: Rihanna

As much as her sound intrigues me, I can't deny that a good part of my interest in Rihanna is visual. With those narrow, pale eyes — like a green visor cutting into the face — Rihanna is extraordinary-looking: one of the great photographic subjects, on a level with Marlene Dietrich and Louise Brooks. A sullen, unsmiling woman in a world of eager starlets, her face is completely closed. How can anyone so ubiquitous be so unreadable? Inscrutability may be her most prized asset.

Importantly, her voice is as implacable as her looks: her sound is the equivalent of that drop-dead sparse beauty. While others reach for high chords and sincerity, Rihanna simply swats at the notes with her heavy butch voice, her powerfully uninflected tone coasting over love songs without need or longing. However, her singing has often been panned for its perceived lack of effort and nuance. Critical concerns over Rihanna came to a head in 2016, with the release of the lead single from her album *Anti*, featuring Drake: a song titled *Work*, no less.

In his *New York Times* review, Jon Caramanica describes *Work* as "a pop-dancehall number that's all bubble and no depth, it's cheaply effective. In places, she barely even relies on words, truncating her syllables past patois to something far less exact." "Cheap" is a key term here: presumably, a more expensive-sounding track would display obvious literacy, evidence of precision and depth, and — weirdly enough — a clean articulation of one's syllables. Cheapness (especially when combined with efficacy, in an unforgivable double blow) is a criticism commonly directed at pop songs, which tend to occupy the lowest rank of aesthetic pleasures.

But the charge that follows the Bajan singer most often is laziness, particularly when it comes to the issues of articulacy and pronunciation. *W* magazine summarized the list of complaints against her with the question, "Is she too lazy to enunciate?" *Time* published an open letter asking her to "please use more words" and push herself towards at least "a hint of lyrical ambition" and "personal expressiveness." Nitsuh Abebe characterizes her attitude as "a kind of joyless disinterest," "the dispassionate voice of a bored professional ... halfway through a double shift" who can "dispatch a solid pop hit, then grab a few hours' sleep before the next day's appointments."

For Caramanica, Rihanna is merely a celebrity "who sometimes, y'know, makes music or whatever"; he refers to one of her songs as "determinedly sloppy." You can read any number of reviews that equate Rihanna's slangy delivery on *Work* with sloth. It is a strange conflation — as if clear diction and the ability to extend one's vowels were the signs of a serious artist.

Perhaps it is Rihanna's cool pose of indifference that leads critics to doubt her work ethic; she does not exhibit the strain and muscle of a Beyoncé or Adele. While Drake comes across as coherent and yearning on *Work*, Rihanna is impenetrable, obdurate. Her repeated enunciation of "I hope" sounds more like a "whoop," closer to an assertion than an aspiration — it does not cede ground or take her off-balance. And she is utterly affectless on the minimal *Pour it Up* (2013), a still presence in the midst of decadence:

the nihilist who encourages revelers to "throw it up, throw it up" as she watches the city go down.

We Found Love (2011), Rihanna's collaboration with Calvin Harris, describes a crash-and-burn affair from which her voice alone emerges unscathed. She sings the phrase "We found love in a hopeless place" close to twenty times, until the repetition of "hopeless" becomes helpless — as senseless as the feeling that drove it. A once-urgent love has become merely reflexive, but as a result it is now unstoppable; the singer is locked on autopilot, reduced to reciting the same mantra as its meaning falls away. The British singer Leona Lewis was originally set to record the track, but her tender, plangent vocals may not have been the right match for Harris: Rihanna's voice here is pure propulsion rather than emotion, buoyed by the song's "stupid" momentum and its intoxicating ride. Once again, critics were put off by the lack of lyrical variety: Jody Rosen of *Rolling Stone* found its repetitions "insipid" and "much ado about very little indeed," while ruefully noting that "it will probably top the Hot 100 anyway."

Making the link between cheapness and success, producer L.A. Reid has likened Rihanna's voice to Coca-Cola: another brand based on a ubiquitous yet inimitable formula, delivering a sure hit of satisfaction each time. But just as the taste of Coca-Cola — overfamiliar yet somehow unrepeatable, inexhaustible — is difficult to pinpoint, the charm of Rihanna's voice is not easy to explain. What seems to be the rote sound of our times turns out to be mysterious and multivocal. This is especially the case on *Work*, where the lyrics consist of Caribbean patois cut in with US slang. According to linguist Lisa Jansen, Rihanna has a "multilingual pop identity," since she "neither sticks to one particular accent (e.g. Bajan or American English) throughout the entire song, nor does she use any of them consistently. Although she uses some of the most prominent Caribbean features in Work, they are not specifically or uniquely Bajan." For Jansen, Rihanna is a singer who "draws on various varieties and eclectically builds her own linguistic repertoire."

The accusations of sloppiness leveled at Work's lyrics only draw attention to the song's slippery pleasures. Instead of a militant "work, work," Rihanna pronounces the chorus as "wur." In fact, the song is one long whir of blurred motion. As "dirt" becomes "dur" and "learn" turns to "lur," Rihanna makes the same sound over and over, retaining the thrust of the word while unscrewing the consonants at either end. Her voice is like taffy, and these loose mouth movements become wonderfully addictive, imprinting themselves on our awareness more than any single word. As Rihanna puts it, "You get what I'm saying but it's not all the way perfect. Because that's how we speak in the Caribbean ... you can understand everything someone means without even finishing the words." There is no better tribute to the confounding power of pop, which generates meanings that defy verbal exactitude.

With the elision of sounds comes a feeling of effortlessness and approximation. Throughout her career, Rihanna has tended to use "nah nah" as a kind of ellipse — a gesture of impatience with no denial implied. Whether saying "nah nah," "yeah, yeah," or "eh, eh" (the latter is particularly memorable in Umbrella), Rihanna doesn't so much sing as bluntly bat at the sound, giving it a forceful downstroke.

In Rude Boy (2010), "nah nah" shuts off a long speech just before the chorus, while the cat-like swipe of "yeah, yeah" sees her marking time, her voice rubbery and unrelenting. At the outset, the singer casually summons a "rude boy" (a Jamaican term for street tough) for sex, and assesses him frankly ("Is you big enough?"). Although the rude boy is chosen for his roughness, the narrator sounds as if she might be a thug herself, snorting and making brassy honking sounds ("want, want, want" is pronounced "wah, wah, wah"). Hurriedly, she tries to get him to the point ("Like, boom boom boom") and is annoyed when he gets the timings wrong ("Relax, let me do it how I wanna"). Her attitude is steely and pragmatic; the much-criticized use of Autotune only emphasizes the robotic and reflexive nature of desire.

Rude Boy is Rihanna's voice at its most ungiving and unproductive, dominated by the careless repetition of "yeah, yeah," but her tone can be even more arresting when paired with a conventional form. In *Diamonds* (2012), Rihanna takes on a song by Sia, the prolific Australian songwriter known for her inspirational numbers. Listen to Sia singing her version of the track: it sounds like an anthem of hard-won validation, with Sia's voice trying to persuade us that we all deserve a place in the firmament, "beautiful like diamonds in the sky." But not for Rihanna the plea for self-affirmation: notice how her "shine bright like a diamond" actually seems to wink out light, as a closed statement rather than a suggestion. In Rihanna's version, we think of the brilliance and hardness of jewels; her tone is eerily cold when it comes to describing "a vision of ecstasy." Her voice cleans away all of the histrionics associated with the power ballad, leaving us with the ice and stark white of diamonds.

Given a song of love or empowerment, Rihanna's voice maintains its characteristic belligerence and tensile strength. Even on her breakthrough single, *SOS* (2006), her "someone help me" was less of a supplication than a demand, a realistic request in the face of a tainted love. The song sounds like a tough-minded reckoning, given the hint of a snarl and the rock phrasing she tends to use for pop songs. I doubt if *SOS* would have been as successful sung by the artist it was originally intended for, the much more ingratiating Christina Milian. Rihanna's tone makes few concessions to the listener. Her flexi-voice, with its superior Teflon quality, cuts through the excess and emotionalism required of most female pop singers.

In the trap song *Bitch Better Have My Money* (2015), Rihanna keeps her lines short and severe, the unchanging blare of her voice serving a flat ultimatum: "Pay me what you owe me!" The single has been controversial; while the anger of the lyrics is directed at the man who ripped her character off, the video seems to get more mileage out of mistreating his wife. Even though captions claim that the male accountant is the bitch of the title, the energy of the clip lies in seeing the relish with which Rihanna strips and brutalizes his trophy wife, accompanied by a gang of vigilante girls. Is yanking the privileges of the man's "bitch" a way of seizing his assets, a form of revenge in kind?

Who is Rihanna in this song? *Bitch Better Have My Money* re-appropriates the misogynist AMG track of the same name, without entirely discarding its view of gender. Together, the video and the merciless tone of Rihanna's voice suggest a character fixated on her male nemesis, yet not above the pleasures of torturing his "bitch." It is the kind of all-encompassing rage seen in Michelle Pfeiffer's Catwoman in *Batman Returns* (1992), who slashes at both an assailant and a damsel in distress, with equal contempt. For now, punishing the bitch's bitch is an acceptable revenge. Violence is splattered like gunfire ("brap, brap, brap"), not discriminating between subjects.

The intractability of Rihanna's voice has been a major factor in her success. In her career-defining hit *Umbrella*, it was her stoic, unyielding "eh, eh" that remained haunting, rather than the perfunctory invitation "You can always come into me." (In the mid-2000s, aspiring female stars released a rash of records titled *Loose, BareNaked, So Sexy, Promiscuous* — anything less than overt was considered uncommercial, such was the mood of the times.) Listeners were also entranced by the way the chorus shaved slices off an umbrella, resulting in a mysteriously curled and repeated sound ("ella, ella"), as if the speaker had lost focus and become attracted to the tail-end of the word. That soft, tendril-like "ella" subsequently hardened into pellets: "eh, eh," the nonchalant bleat that has been her vocal signature ever since.

That Rihanna's restraint is a choice has been amply demonstrated by *FourFiveSeconds* (2015) and *Love on the Brain* (2016): two affecting singles that happen to fit classical structures and models of good singing. Paired with Kanye West and Paul McCartney on *FourFiveSeconds*, she is easily the most striking vocalist on the track: her bruised delivery and the very precise inflections of husk and edge (she pronounces "kindness" with a sharp warning tone) ensure that the song never becomes mawkish. Performing with West and McCartney at the Grammys in 2015, Rihanna dominated the song with her deliberate vocal shadings, the hard triangle of her mouth, and her staunch body position — even Kanye seemed recessive by comparison.

On the doo-wop ballad *Love On The Brain*, a standout on the album *Anti*, Rihanna uses different parts of her range for each section of the track — one might even mistake her work for that of multiple vocalists. In the first verse, the tissue-thin delicacy of her voice is a tone we rarely hear from the singer. This serenade is as close to beseeching as Rihanna will get: fluttery and unguarded, with just a hint of rugged texture. However, the chorus returns with a swagger and a tougher level of talk: her voice has that indestructible, metallic quality we more commonly associate with Rihanna. By coming back with a markedly different sound — potentially a new persona, or at least a change of heart — the singer shows us that the emotional emphasis has shifted. The fragile tribute of the verse has met with a reality check, a mood of seasoned resignation. The chorus only returns to the light, breathy voice for a single word ("brain"), before heading into the despair of the second verse. For those who have questioned Rihanna's willingness to "give it up" — or her ability to do so — *Love On The Brain* should act as a reprieve.

But even though Rihanna has proved she can do soul and warmth with the best of them, she is at her most striking and distinctive when her voice is difficult to process. It may be the shifting meanings of "nah nah" that engross us, or the mix of Jamaican, Bajan, and American accents that makes words hard to decipher yet instantly impactful. There is the hard-boiled "uh" sound that resembles a male grunt, the heads-up "yay-yo, yay-yo" that puts the listener on notice. Her best songs are based on a hypnotic repetition of "nonsense" sounds that some find cheap, others enchanting. The miracle of *Umbrella* is that we are prepared to spend three staid verses waiting for a trace of that sound: "ella, ella," the edge of an echo carved into space.

Nicki Minaj: The Laughter in Madness

The Mae West of our times, Nicki is both girlie and self-deprecating, cartoonish and alarming, preening yet ironic. Happy to market herself as a plastic Barbie, along with the mature woman she is, Nicki is pop's goddess of many faces, many voices. Moving between a variety of Cockney, Californian, and Trinidadian accents, she has several defined alter egos: the most famous being Roman Zolanski, a gay Jewish man with rage issues, and Roman's mother Martha, the British housewife determined to straighten out her boy. In between are the hybrid selves that see Nicki merging with Marilyn Monroe, Anna Nicole Smith, and Monica Lewinsky to form new identities, enhanced versions of the sexpots of the last century.

In the track that made her reputation, Kanye West's *Monster* (2010), Nicki invents a feral twin to terrorize her pink Barbie self. She switches her voice between banshee and baby doll with — why not? — a bit of Cockney thrown in, since Barbie's accent turns unaccountably English later on. While the banshee's voice shivers with anger, she is also unexpectedly worldly, dropping the names of designer labels ("Monster Giuseppe heel, that's the monster shoe") and even flaunting her friendship with the rapper M.I.A. ("a bad bitch that came from Sri Lanka") as an accessory.

A smug little princess, Barbie seems to get her stereotypes of cuteness confused, sliding from preppy L.A. into full-on Spice Girl. When the Barbie dares to pipe up with some legitimate questions about Nicki's star power — and gets in a few boasts of her own — the banshee threatens to rip her apart, culminating in a hellraising scream. All this within the space of one verse!

Nicki's portion of *Monster* is so jammed with idiosyncrasies that we can't help but be disappointed when the track returns to a lone male speaker, who expresses a single point of view. Blasting us from monster to baby and back, she easily eclipses Kanye and the song's other collaborators: Rick Ross, Jay-Z, and Bon Iver. Nicki's verse has so much on its mind — surprising us with changes in tone, rhythm, and persona — that the other singers' lines seem tame and linear: workmanlike at best, meekly chugging along to the beat.

Arguably, Nicki's greatest work has been as a featured performer on the tracks of other artists — definitively on *Monster*, but also on Trey Songz's *Bottoms Up* (2010), the single remix of Big Sean's *Dance (A$$)* in 2011, and Swizz Beatz's *Hands Up* (2013). Her presence works best when it is hotly anticipated — her appearance often comes late in the song, as the coup of a special guest star. In *Bottoms Up*, her entry is positioned as a final burst of originality before the return of the chorus, when the dull slog of Songz's voice sets in. In her verse, Nicki veers between a helpless infant who wants to be spoon-fed cocktails and innuendo ("Could I get that salt around that rim rim rim?"), a stern businesswoman, and the voice that zestily yells, "Fuck her! Fuck her! Fuck her!" The mercurial Nicki shows up the conventionality of the rest of the track, making its reversion to routine nearly unbearable.

In *Hands Up*, her queenly cameo, dismissing her rivals as children, makes the voices of Swizz Beatz, Lil Wayne, 2 Chainz, and (once again) Rick Ross seem like the humming of so many drones. Post-Nicki, other rappers tend to sound one-dimensional, with their predictable focus on boasting, girls, drinks, or the club experience. On Nicki's own single *Only* (2014), she headlines and holds court while Wayne, Drake, and Chris Brown come to pay tributes. She comes across as powerful, but less exciting than in her guest appearances.

Nicki benefits from compression and urgency: when she is forced to condense all of her voices and eccentricities into the limits of one verse. Some artists work better with restriction than an open canvas or a free hand; Nicki's creativity shines when she is given tiny prisons and parameters, such as the time scheme and subject matter of *Monster*.

Even in a 2018 comic sketch for *Saturday Night Live*, Nicki shows how far she can go with a small, direct brief. The skit starts off as a parody of the band Haim, but she transforms its meaning midway. Given 30 seconds to throw down a rap about female friendship and solidarity, Nicki delivers a breathlessly clean diss, incorporating vicious threats, die-hard loyalty, and even the names of cast members Kate McKinnon, Aidy Bryant, and Tina Fey. She caps it off with a childish, sniggering sound ("Ooh-ooh, ooh-ooh-ooh-ooh"), a taunting boogie that is instantly taken up by the other actors; her gift for rhythm makes the peculiarities of her tone contagious.

While Nicki occasionally plays the toddler, it is her ability to infantilize others that makes her persona so distinctive. As she has claimed on multiple tracks, "All these bitches is my sons": Nicki degrades male competitors by offering to suckle and nurse them. Nurturing is an aggressive act, a way to consolidate a power base and breed a race of followers dependent on her whims. *Did It On'em* (2012) reveals how her ideal family works: "All these bitches is my sons / And Imma go and get some bibs for 'em / A couple formulas, little pretty lids on 'em." Nicki pretends to dote on her rivals as if they were sweet babes, indulging them only to humiliate them with diaper talk. Macho rappers are subjected to an emasculating concern in *Blow Ya Mind* ("Did these niggas fall and bump their little heads?" 2010) and *Born Stunna* ("You my son bitch, and it's bedtime," 2012).

In the Minaj universe, mothering is mastery: a specifically female form of one-upmanship. By declaring herself the mother of all rappers, Nicki claims to be the originator of hip-hop vernacular, an expert speaker watching her sons stutter and mewl. Giving birth means she has ultimate bragging rights, demanding filial piety while threatening to withhold love, care, and even legitimacy ("So fuck a funny style, tryna act hard / Uh, you my son, no daddy, you a bastard ... They talk slick and wondering why I be sonning them" in *Hands Up*). "Sonning" is a method of cutting down to size, in ways only a mother can: in *Give It All To Me* (2013), Nicki is the icy, disapproving mom who can yank away privileges in an instant ("I'm like, 'Who's up?' / Girls is used up / These bitches is my sons, I tied my tubes up"). Boys who misbehave face abuse or disinheritance ("You my son, son prodigal / And you adopted, not even biological"), although in Nicki's take on gender, "sons" can also be female: in *The Boys* (2012), she sings, "Girls is my sons, carried them for eight months / And yes, you're premature" and "Or the razor, yeah the razor / She my son yeah, but I ain't raise her." Where most rappers trade insults about money, sex, and success, Nicki knows that maternal disappointment cuts deeper.

While she embraces the power of mothering and conception, Nicki is not above whipping out a male body part from time to time ("If I had a dick, I would pull it out and piss on 'em," from the polemical *Did It On'em*). Although female parts can be tossed around with considerable swagger ("Give me that damn bucket / When I throw this pussy you better not start duckin'," from *Knockout*, 2010), we hear quite a lot about Nicki's dick, both in and out of her male Roman persona. The singer, who refers to herself as both king and queen, is determined to have the full arsenal of weaponry. Male bodies and voices are used to express a coarser kind of anger — shitting and pissing on hecklers, or anyone who dares to fall out of her slipstream. Still, it is can be unclear whether Nicki is playing man or woman, parent or child, at any given time.

Biology, chronology, sex, and race offer no resistance to this shape-shifting artist: no sooner does she mention a trait than she merges with it, creating a curious form of hybrid personality. Nicki does not merely reference Anna Nicole Smith and Monica Lewinsky, she fuses with them to become the super-entities Anna Nicki and Nicki Lewinsky. Nicki Lewinsky, a character who appears in multiple songs, is an update from the Nineties model, this time with her sexuality weaponized. While Monica Lewinsky has been referenced in numerous rap songs including Eminem's *XL Show Freestyle* (1998), Black Menace's *Block Bleeder* (1999), and Aaron Omar's *It Has Been Said* (2012), mostly in a pejorative context, Minaj's version is a wised-up woman who knows where real power lies. As played by Nicki, this Lewinsky is a world-toppler, in the line of Helen of Troy and Cleopatra; she will never be a punchline or a footnote. A modern Delilah, she makes full use of having the president in her thrall.

This habit of creating personalities through birthing and naming seems to be chronic. In dreamily appropriating the identities of others, her taste is for the hyper-specific — note that her vision of the archetypal Brit is Jewish, Polish, gay, and gender-ambiguous. In the case of Roman Zolanski, Nicki takes on the name of a wildly notorious figure: apparently on phonetic grounds, although with Zolanski, controversy is never far off. Much has been made of the incongruity of a Trinidad-born, Queens-raised woman singing with an English accent, as if it were just a trendy aspect of marketing or being quirky. Not at all: Nicki's Anglophilia runs deep, and Cockney is one of her truest voices, an ideal channel for her bawdy humor and campness. You haven't lived until you've heard Nicki on *American Idol*, flirting with a handsome contestant ("my baby daddy"), speaking American slang in a voice that is purest geezer.

Over the years, Nicki's magpie mind has seized on various bits of Englishness, from the voice of Oxford-educated Emma Watson to the Dick Van Dyke of *Mary Poppins*, by way of various chavs and Spice Girls, to come up with her Anglo ideal. She now has a glory box of characters, both broad and nuanced, which she continues to add to and evolve. The English voice has completely fused with her personality, and it is surprisingly flexible, not reliant on stock phrases or clichés. Her take on Cockney certainly ranks above Kate Bush's.

Who's to say that this English Nicki isn't as fully lived and authentic as her American self? Or even her Afro-Caribbean self? Although she was born in Saint James and raised by a Trinidadian mother in New York, Nicki has often been criticized for using slang from Jamaica rather than Trinidad, and for not being "Trini enough." For those who regard cultural fusion as an irritating tic, note that Nicki makes a much more convincing Englishwoman than she does a Caribbean; to Trinidadian critics, her "roots" seems manufactured. She moves freely between regional tones, Received English, and patois, with an authorial assurance that reminds one of Salman Rushdie.

It is the natural way of the magpie, the bowerbird, the imitative lyrebird, to pick up glittery fragments of language and possess them fully. Growing up in Queens must have been a feast for the ear, with its range of regional and mixed-island accents, but there's no evidence that Nicki was more attracted to these voices than the ones from trans-Atlantic pop culture. As we have seen earlier, she has the ability to inhabit and become whatever she describes. With her sci-fi-like division and multiplication of selves, Minaj might be the only actor who could replace Tatiana Maslany if the series *Orphan Black* were to be rejigged as a comedy.

In her lyrics, Nicki gravitates towards shiny, exciting words, whatever tastes fresh in the mouth. On their track *Mercy* (2012), Lil Wayne is content with name-checking Lamborghinis and Mercedes, but Nicki's version of luxury is to conjure a paradise of exotic phrases: "Diablo, Alejandro, dimelo, Gandhi!" In the interests of rhyme, "dashiki" will be paired with "Waikiki," added to the storehouse of melodic words, along with Harajuku, Svengali, and even Mandingo! Despite its title, *Coco Chanel* (2018) is less about designer threads than talking in tongues, with a Spanish-language chorus that somehow segues into Japanese and Chinese names, before a Gurkha pops up out of nowhere. Even when describing her "own" US culture, her voice pops across the Atlantic to sample it as an outsider ("You know, I really got a thing for American guys" in *Super Bass*, 2011).

It might be said that, like the British-Swedish-American Neneh Cherry, Nicki has more reasons to contain multiple voices than most: that she has her background to thank for the grab of her imagination, the way she eats up and digests other personalities. But the extent to which those voices are fused is a model for modern identity, in which one naturally inhabits a cluster of styles, periods, and languages. Despite their breadth, her references are densely woven together, no mere mash-up; her characters are linked by a delirious run of associations, both sonic and verbal.

Nicki's multi-vocal identity highlights the unpredictability of what the ear retains, or shuts out – whether it be an overheard snippet of TV, or the sound of one's immediate environment. There is no telling what the artist, the listener, will be drawn into. Magazines will often publish a musician's list of impeccably curated influences, featuring a token mix of respectable and diverse names. But an artist may have only the faintest awareness of what their influences really are. It may only be a single syllable that has triggered imaginative investment: a crisp voice heard on the radio, an accent absorbed from a book.

There is no word, no milieu, no status that Nicki cannot make her own. In her music, and in her resplendent photo shoots, she has shown us, time and again, that there is no novelty in black aristocracy; she creates a new classicism, no longer tied to pallor or restraint. We are never sure where her voice is "coming from," geographically or emotionally — whether a tremor signals a move into vibrato Englishness, or the return of her gothic *Monster* voice. All of history is available for Nicki to use. She does not accept the view that she is marginalized, excluded, or anything less than a privileged sampler of the world's cultures — a quality she has in common with Azealia Banks.

All of Them Anomalies

With her penchant for normalizing the outrageous, I believe the visionary fashion editor Diana Vreeland would have adored Nicki, Rihanna, and Azealia. In her famous "Why Don't You?" column — a list of preposterous ideas delivered with practical ease — and her motto "Pink is the navy blue of India," Vreeland proposed that what seemed ridiculous to you might only be realism for others. She relished a reversal of context to show up the narrowness of social expectations.

Like Nicki, Vreeland was beyond affectation: there was no clash between immersive fantasy and public performance. If shocking pink was the new norm, then our conventional understanding of space, time, genetics, and common sense might fade away into navy blue.

Pink happens to be Nicki Minaj's default setting. As with Azealia Banks and Rihanna, her taste for the diverse is instinctive rather than just for show. Her work happens to be multicultural, but it is not weakened by pleas for tolerance and inclusivity. Her performance style is both camply retro and boldly futuristic, lampooning the generic nature of authority: for instance, toting a random white man as her own personal Pope to the Grammys. Musically, visually, and imaginatively, Nicki's domain is the unlikely made plausible. Her "authentic" artistic identity is a composite of different accents and alter egos, with the result that we don't always know who is speaking.

In the song *Roman Holiday* (2012), once Nicki is done voicing Roman's strident mother, urging him to take a break "from your sanity," she digs deep into the character of Roman. But Roman himself consists of multiple voices, among them a tough talker, an introverted sadist, and a fashionista. Nicki nails the uncertainty around his (and her own) personalities when she sings, "Who the fuck is this hoe? And yes, maybe just a touch of Tourette's." However, it is clear that she has fully internalized his confusion, and not only verbally. Two lines of this verse are purely jerked breath: anger that hasn't made it into words, which can only be expressed rhythmically. Today, many artists talk the talk when it comes to identity and gender fluidity, but Nicki embodies and enacts what she describes.

Vreeland once said that her idea of utopia was "a garden in hell," and I can't think of a better description for the aesthetics of Nicki and Azealia: that mixture of perversion and paradise that both are driven towards. These two artists, like Neneh Cherry before them, have made the abject cozy and livable, taking it to the very center of popular culture. As peculiar as they are, both have staked their claim as the voice of the mainstream, rather than marginalized experience.

Inevitably, bringing such concerns into the world of pop music will strike some as pretentious. After all, who do they think they are? So much of the public dialogue around these women regards them as poseurs: cultural samplers without any roots to show. But with superb authorial arrogance, Nicki and Azealia remind us that the world of mythology is as much theirs as the ground beneath their feet. It is a lesson hybrid girls might take to heart.

(LOVE IS) THE POWER OF OOH

You're History focuses on female artists who are utterly in the mainstream of culture, but remain peculiar in ways that haven't been fully discussed or acknowledged. These are performers whose songs have become so ubiquitous that their structural oddity is now hard to apprehend — from an obvious banger such as Janet Jackson's *What Have You Done for Me Lately*, to the early Nineties singles of TLC, enduringly popular among teen audiences, to those two mainstays of dancefloors, Chaka Khan's *Ain't Nobody* and *I Feel For You*.

Although Khan, TLC, and increasingly, Jackson have received critical respect, their songs are seldom described in detail, partly because so much of their impact is about the simmering, concentrated "ooh," the cooling and relieving effect of the "aah." Given the rationalizing impulse that dominates writing on popular music, ecstatic sensations like these are often passed over. Historically, rock journalism has tended to carry a pose of knowingness, of placing and summarizing work rather than being overwhelmed or struggling to make sense of sounds. It also has a tradition of being resistant to immediate pleasure — particularly melodic pleasure — treating it as an object of suspicion rather than fascination or mystery.

But mystery is an essential factor in the appreciation of pop: *Why* am I so struck by this sound? What is it I can't get out of my head? Rather than dismissal or camp indulgence, a more useful approach to pop may be puzzlement: at its lingering effects, the felicities or contradictions offered by its rhythms and its utterances. Listening intensely to pop is about exploring compulsion and its reasons: the conviction that any sound that stops us in our tracks is worthy of curiosity. Why does that tacky-sounding synth make a mark I can't erase? How is that "ooh" so specifically suggestive, to the point of obscenity? Without that kind of attention, many key aspects of the artists in this book will not be of interest: the sour sounds of Neneh Cherry, the aggressive use of synth in Kate Bush and Janet Jackson, the grating and harsh notes struck by Azealia Banks and Siobhan Fahey.

In these artists we find a range of perverse pleasures, alongside the warmer, more sensual delights offered by Khan and Sade. Make no mistake, pop is a pleasure party — even if its treats can be of the uncanny variety, such as the icy hardness of sound savored by Cherry, Banks, and often Taylor Swift. Aesthetic enjoyment is the one thing that's indispensable to the genre.

The critic Judith Williamson once wrote that the problem she had with highly theoretical films by directors such as Peter Wollen, as opposed to mainstream movies, was that all the ideas were "easily separable from the action." Although intelligently constructed, Wollen's films failed to touch a nerve because his ideas were communicated without "producing pleasure." Pleasure is what enables the values of art and music to be absorbed, beyond self-consciousness. When a song generates coherent messages that are easily separable from its sounds and rhythms, it begs the question: Why need music? The greatest songs are those whose meanings could *only* be released through music, where the lyrics are laid down in some odd or beguiling pattern, in which no note can be replaced. That underlying pattern is what grips, and gives us mysteries to decode forever.

I will cite another excellent critic, Emily Nussbaum, whose work in *New York* magazine and *The New Yorker* has been trailblazing in the serious study of television. In the Nineties, Nussbaum had trouble convincing her fellow arts grads to pay critical attention to TV that was fun, pop, and often driven by female characters. She found that particular hierarchies were "embedded (and often, hidden) in questions of aesthetics ... What kind of person got to be a genius? Whose story counted as universal? Which type of art had staying power?"

Today, thanks to the work of writers like Nussbaum, irresistible pop pleasures such as *The Unbreakable Kimmy Schmidt* are discussed with the same interest and rigor as epic crime sagas. In this so-called "golden age" of TV, most critics know better than to write off addictive, enjoyable shows as guilty pleasures. However, for the most part, the analysis of music continues to venerate the work of "ideas," the erudite lyric over the specifically impassioned cry of "ooh." If we dismiss the genius of Chaka Khan's "Oh-oh-oh-ohhh" or Janet Jackson's "ooh-ooh-ooh, yeah" on literary grounds, then we ignore the potency of music as a medium in itself.

But the mysterious power behind those sublime sounds is still waiting to be unleashed: paradise is there for taking. I swear on a stack of albums — and the greatest "oohs" of all time — that the mystery is worth pursuing.

APPENDIX
THE DEVIL IN LOVE:
THE GREATEST OOHS IN MODERN MUSIC

1. Prince, *Gett Off* (1991)

The squeals and yelps of Prince could alone fill this entire list. From the cat-in-heat yowl that triggers *Cream* (1991) to the final shattering cry of *Thieves in the Temple* (1990), each one is as specific as a fragrance note, opening up an emotional register inaccessible to language. One of the richest and strangest must be the ear-splitting sound at the start of *Gett Off*, when the master of decadence introduces us to his lair. It is a piercing shriek that devolves into a whining, nagging noise, as if the master were at the mercy of his own whims: seducing guests before being put through the wringer himself. Prince is both the lothario and the slave to love: we are inducted into a world of pleasure, but with odd notes of terror and pleading in it.

2. Ray Charles, *What'd I Say* (1959)

It was the non-lexical sounds, rather than the lyrics, which sparked bans on US radio — not surprising when you hear the hunger and urgency behind those moans by Charles and The Raelettes. Three minutes in, Charles senses the controversy ahead and wants to end the song; he has to be pushed by his entourage ("Don't quit now!" "C'mon, honey!") to keep going. He and The Raelettes respond with a series of back-and-forth groans ("Ohhhh!" "Ohhhh!") that become increasingly frenzied. Charles thrills to their culmination with a final, crackling "Ohh!," and later "Aah!"

and "Wooah"! All this commotion and carry-on over a song in which a man merely seeks clarification! ("Tell me what'd I say?") As Stephen King defined certain objects as "needful things" — those that seek satisfaction through human action — Ray Charles' "Ohhhh!" is the best example of a needful sound, a cry that demands satiation.

3. The Emotions, *Best of My Love* (1977)

Is there a pop moment more paradisiacal than the climax of this song? Co-written by Maurice White of Earth, Wind & Fire, its outro floods us with non-verbal sounds and the feeling of bliss. From the cruisy "whoa, whoa" of the chorus and the "ow!" just after the final bridge, The Emotions build to a euphoric, floor-to-ceiling release: "Ohhhhhhh!" The Hutchinson sisters sing it with exalted arms and eyes cast up to high heaven, then mark the song's descent with a series of ecstatic popping "ohs."

4. Sister Sledge, *He's the Greatest Dancer* (1979)

Despite the roll-call of designer names and looks, what really elevates this song — giving it a sudden surge in energy levels — is the "Oh what, wow!" of the chorus. With its sound of whiplash, "Oh what, wow!" sets off a mental flash and flare better than any descriptive phrase could. It evokes a lightning bolt, a small burst of sensation like disco's signature move, the diagonal arm pump (which I have seen sign language interpreters use as shorthand for "John Travolta").

5. Pink Floyd, *The Great Gig in the Sky* (1973)

Although the ostensible subject of this song is the fear of death, the impact of the vocals is much more immediate:

Clare Torry's wailing hits the gut level of pain. That pang has inspired at least two masterworks, from the Marco Bellocchio film *Buongiorno, Notte* (2003), where it marks the protagonist's switch of sympathy, to Peeping Tom's brilliant theater piece *Le Salon* (2004). In the latter, Torry's cry is heard as we realize that a father prefers to prey on his daughter rather than have sex with his no-longer-nubile wife. We feel the kick inside: the unbelievable sensation that capsizes the body.

6. Earth, Wind & Fire, *Let's Groove* (1981)

No-one knew more about the power of "ooh" to signal an energy transfer than Maurice White. On the band's earlier single, *September* (1978), White fought for the primacy of non-verbal sounds. Against his fellow songwriters, he refused to replace the "ba-dee-ya" of the chorus with "real words," knowing that those three syllables — if sung with enough conviction — could express the incoherence of longing.

The chorus of *Let's Groove* offers clipped inducements to dance, but it is the bridge, with its series of transformative "oohs," which activates the change: "Just *moooove* yourself ... And *lo-ooh-ooh-se* yourself." It is the softening effect of the "ooh" that gets us from A to B, taking us from the staccato verse to a state of extreme swoon: "*moooove.*" With the body in cruise control, the song now tells us to "*gliiide* like a 747." The result was a groove so irresistible it defied the anti-disco movement of the Eighties (which sought to cleanse music of funk and return it to order via rock) to become a major hit.

7. Chic, *Le Freak* (1978)

It's technically an "aahhh," but this is the sound synonymous with disco: the long upward slurp that precedes "Freak out!" It is a cry mysteriously suggestive of obedience. Try singing it: putting all the stress on the start of the "aahhh" forces you to incline your head, before a sudden uptick at the end.

8. Soft Cell, *Tainted Love* (1981)

When Gloria Jones' original version of *Tainted Love* was released in 1964, the chorus ("Whoa, tainted love") was not the song's highlight: the "whoa" was surprised, disapproving, but unspectacular. The single was a flop. But on Soft Cell's cover, that line is indelible: "Ohhhh... tainted love." As Marc Almond's voice drains away, "Ohhhh" is the sound of ruin: of the lover not only disappointed but utterly appalled, scandalized at his betrayal. In the accusing verses, Almond gives a hint of sulky punk delivery, but it is the "Ohhhh" that puts an ugly stain on love, the note of dismay we all remember.

9. Toni Braxton, *You're Makin' Me High* (1996)

This track contains as many references to high/low and hot/cold as a Cole Porter tune. *You're Makin' Me High* is made to showcase Braxton's lower register, as the rare alto among pop divas. The chorus begins with "Ooh, I get so high" when her own voice is cello-deep; counter-intuitively, she sings "You make my temperature rise" as the melodic line descends. On the title phrase, her voice hits an apex on "high" before shuddering down to its depths.

Braxton's tone is often muted: sighing and muttering sexual invitations amid the talk of "heart and soul." For the most part, she uses her voice quite sparingly, letting the backing vocals do the heavy lifting. This puts the focus on her timbre, as she applies little touches of that buttery richness here and there. This is a song made up of smoldering "oohs" and cooling "ahs," every high and low a form of temperature control.

10. Rufus and Chaka, *Any Love* (1979)

Although eclipsed by the success of *Do You Love What You Feel* (1979) and *I'm Every Woman* (1978) at the time, *Any Love* may be the greatest track on Rufus and Chaka Khan's seminal *Masterjam* (1979). It also demonstrates that what a song chooses to talk about may be the last thing it wants to explore.

The lyrics of this song don't add up: the chorus and bridge evoke the pain and heartbreak of relationships, while the verses refer to a single man on the margins, barely able to score eye contact let alone a date. There hardly appears to be a protagonist here — merely a series of observations and wishes with no linkage. But it doesn't matter at all: the lack of lyrical coherence only shows up what this song is really about. It is, in fact, "about" vibrato: the reverberations of Khan's voice, which lift and carry us through the track.

The opening describes a guy who unsuccessfully skims the dating scene — but then, without warning, the chorus plunges us into the epic emotions of an affair, ending with a rueful "ohhhhh," the long wave-like sound that dominates the track. Since the chorus is a springboard for that echoing note of recrimination, its lyrics describe betrayal and loss. However, when we return to the verse, it's as if that dynamic never existed — we're back to the club scene and being single again. Passion disappears until the next iteration of the chorus.

The emotions in this track are clearly cut and chosen to showcase Khan's amazing vibrato, dispensing with narrative as needed. That is the song's real and only "subject": the extraordinary resonance of its "ohhhhh."

INDEX

TOM
WHYMAN

INFINITELY
FULL OF HOPE

*FATHERHOOD AND THE FUTURE IN
AN AGE OF CRISIS AND DISASTER*

REPEATER BOOKS

is dedicated to the creation of a new reality. The landscape of twenty-first-century arts and letters is faded and inert, riven by fashionable cynicism, egotistical self-reference and a nostalgia for the recent past. Repeater intends to add its voice to those movements that wish to enter history and assert control over its currents, gathering together scattered and isolated voices with those who have already called for an escape from Capitalist Realism. Our desire is to publish in every sphere and genre, combining vigorous dissent and a pragmatic willingness to succeed where messianic abstraction and quiescent co-option have stalled: abstention is not an option: we are alive and we don't agree.